AF646453

CASTEISM IN INDIAN POLITICS

CASTEISM IN INDIAN POLITICS

Dasarathi Bhuyan

ANMOL PUBLICATIONS PVT. LTD.
NEW DELHI - 110 002 (INDIA)

ANMOL PUBLICATIONS PVT. LTD.
H.O.: 4374/4B, Ansari Road, Darya Ganj,
New Delhi-110 002 (India)
Ph.: 23278000, 23261597
B.O.: No. 1015, Ist Main Road, BSK IIIrd Stage
IIIrd Phase, IIIrd Block,
Bangalore - 560 085 (India)
Visit us at: www.anmolpublications.com

Casteism in Indian Politics

© Reserved

First Published, 2006

ISBN 81-261-2850-X

[Responsibility for the facts stated, opinions expressed, conclusions reached and plagiarism, if any, in this book is entirely that of the Author. The Publishers bear no responsibility for them, whatsoever.]

PRINTED IN INDIA

Printed at Mehra Offset Press, Delhi.

Contents

Preface

Social inequalities are a universal feature in social structure. The fact that inequality varies considerably in form, function and scope from one society to another, indicates that these features are not uniform. In Indian society the inequality is manifested in terms of caste. Indians are divided into thousands of castes. Caste is a peculiarly Indian institution, which has no counterpart elsewhere. Studies of Bailey, Rajani Kothari, Srinivas identified caste as one of the major integrative elements of Indian social structure. The process of industrialisation, urbanization, modernization, sanskritization, and westernization has loosen the grasp of caste system. But the evil system of caste still persists in Indian society. Caste continues to be a major determinant of political participation in India. Jaya Prakash Narayan once observed that the caste had become most important political party in India. All political parties give great weightage to the caste factor in selecting their candidate, in allocating constituencies to their candidates and in canvassing support for their nominees in the elections. It also plays a basic role in the decision making process. Caste-based violence very often finds its way into politics. The situation is often met with violent attacks by high caste groups on low-caste groups. Though the spirit of secularism stands clearly affirmed in the Indian constitution, yet it recognizes the caste system in the form of providing for the reservation of seats for scheduled castes and scheduled tribes. The emergence of strong pro-reservation and anti-reservation groups in India has been the direct consequence of these provisions of the constitution. The above account clearly illustrates the dominant role of caste in Indian politics.

This volume attempts to assess the role of caste in Indian politics since its origin to the present. In chapter-10, I have tried to show the result of my study "caste as the determinant of political participation."

In last part I have suggested some steps to check casteism. To eliminate casteism must be our first and top priority. All Indians as true sons and daughters of motherland must come forward to fight against casteism.

I hope this book will be of great interest to students of social sciences, researchers, educators, politicians, academicians, and sociologists not only to understand the problem of casteism but also resolve the evils of casteism.

While writing the present work, I have extensively quoted from various books, magazines the related paragraphs. I show my gratitude to all those who had been a source of help. In spite of all these precautions if I have faulted somewhere, I tender my unconditional apology for the same.

—Dasarathi Bhuyan

1

Meaning and Definition of Caste

Caste is an Indian institution and has no parlance elsewhere. Caste continues to be a major determinant of political life in India. Caste has deep roots in the Indian social system and social structure. Various studies on Indian Politics show the significant role, which have been played in the process of power capturing. A systematic analysis of the origin of caste system indicates that there are many theories, which explain its origin and development. Traditional, racial, religious and occupational theories of origin and development of the caste system occupy an important place in sociological literature.

The virus of caste has percolated to all sectors of human life. Indians are divided into thousands of caste, sub-caste and tribes. Even after half a century of India's Independence castes play a divisive factor in Indian social fabric and obstruct India's unity and emotional integration. In India there is a proverbial saying that everything changes in India except the caste. It has been more pronounced in rural areas of Indian society. The adherence of caste system has been less pronounced in urban areas as compared to its rural counterparts. The Constitution of India has endeavoured to establish a secular, socialistic and democratic society in India. In spite of the declaration of these principles by Indian Constitution after independence Indian society is traditional one. The process of industrialisation, urbanization and modernization has loosen the grasp of caste system and other old values. The traditional values are still their significant role in the structure and function of contemporary Indian society in general and rural areas in particular. Presence of castes as one of the most ancient features of Indian society has been naturally acting as a major factor of Indian political system. It acts, as J.P. Narayan once observed, the most major political party in India. It has been determinant of political participation, voting behavior and almost all other aspects of Indian politics.

Caste determines the nature, organisation and working of political parties and interest groups, legislatures and bureaucratic and in fact all political structures and their function, caste-based voting, caste-based candidatures, caste-based riots, "Wars," caste conflicts and the issue of reservation versus non-reservations are all factors of Indian politics. All this makes the study of role of caste in the functioning of Indian politics and imperative necessity for every student of Indian Political System. Many social scientists like Srinivas, Rajani Kothari, Ram Ashray Rai, Y. Singh, T.K. Oommen, G.S. Ghurye, and Iravati Karve has already undertaken researches in which they have established that caste has many ramifications in Indian society and has almost influenced all the areas of the life of Indian citizens in rural areas.

Caste associations and caste federations which have been officially recognized, play a dominant role in strengthening their position and also in the political process. Moreover, caste has been politicized with the introduction of parliamentary system of Government, right to vote and periodic elections. The electoral behavior and voting pattern are determined by caste considerations. Nomination of candidates by political parties and the voting campaign on caste lines are influenced at the instance of various caste associations. This gives rise to fighting among the regional caste – lobbies which ultimately end in caste conflict and caste tension. Caste factor also plays an important role in ministry making.

There are about three thousand castes existing in India. These castes have been exploited by the leaders of political parties and administrators for the attainment of their selfish interests. Some times caste influence to political party and some times political party influences to caste. Political parties and castes influence some times administrators. In the same way the administrators exploit the Political Parties and the castes. Now-a-days Political Parties are contesting local elections. Political Parties are nominating candidates and elections are won on the basis of caste cum Political Party. Thus, caste plays a significant role in politics as well as administration of the rural society where people know each other castes back ground.

It is arguable that caste is now a dying force in structural terms. People of the same caste are engaged in various occupations; People belonging to all castes are seen drinking and smoking; distinction in custom, dress and speech is found more on the basis of rural urban residence, age, sex than caste affiliation. The hold of purity-pollution complex has also slackened over years. In the cities, Brahmins frequently work with non-Brahmins in the same factories, business firms and Government offices. They live in the same neighborhoods and send their children to the same schools, colleges and professional institutions. Though the process of Sanskritization and modernization have cut short the gap between the higher castes and lower castes including the untouchables, but, the situation is often met with violent attacks by high caste groups on low caste groups. Thus, despite these obvious and significant changes, caste is not on its last legs. Rather the economic and political interests have discovered in it an important vehicle to consolidate new values of caste identities. Finally, the division of society on caste lines has given a deathblow to the national integration. Thus the national integration process comes to a grinding halt.

Before going a detail into the subject let us know the meaning of caste.

Meaning of Caste

The word caste has been derived from the Portuguese word 'Casta', which means lineage. Among the Europeans who came to India in the 15th and 16th centuries, the Portuguese appear to have understood the Indian system correctly and applied the appropriate word caste. In Hinduism caste is referred to varna meaning colour.

In Spanish language caste means breed, race, strain or a complex of hereditary qualities. In India the right word is 'Jati'. Caste in India refers to a social stratification. Indian caste system is a perfect social division. It is hierarchical and quite elaborate. As applied to social class systems, the word refers to stratification along lines of descent. That means as individual is born into a given social category and remains there for lifes.

A very eminent sociologist named Ghurye is of the opinion that, a caste has the following important characteristics:

Caste is inborn: A man dies in the same caste in which he is born. The caste determines his social status.

Caste prescribes it's food: A Brahmin should be vegetarian, Kshatriyas and Sudras can take non-vegetarian food, but not allowed to eat beef.

Caste does not allow marriage outside the same caste: Caste is endogamous. This rigid system does not allow an inter-caste marriage. The violation of the rule will lead to expulsion from the caste.

Caste system is hierarchical: There are some upper

castes and some lower castes. The relative position is not interchangeable. In the hierarchy, the Brahmin caste enjoys certain privileges.

Caste occupations are fixed: Every caste has to perform the occupation which is prescribed for it. For example, the Brahmin's job of priesthood can not be transferred to any other caste. The Kshatriyas and Vaisyas are to look after defense and trade. The job of Sudras is to serve the above three other castes.

Caste has its own court or panchayat to punish: If any member of a caste group disobeys the fixed rules, traditions, established customs, he is liable to be punished by the caste panchayat.

Some scholars have argued that caste system have been maintained by many societies throughout history. There are two views among social scientists, especially those who worked in India on caste system. Some scholars argued that the caste system is to be defined in term of its Hindu attributes and rational and therefore, unique to India. There are others who gave the opinion that caste system has to be defined in terms of structural features which are found not only in Hindu India but in a number of society as well. These scholars saw caste group in such widely scattered areas as the Arabian Peninsula, North Africa, East Africa, Japan aboriginal, North America and the contemporary United States of America.

Both opinion are relevant and it depends upon ones interest and purposes of study to accept the one or the other. The concept of Caste or Jati is different from 'Varna.' To a layman 'Varna' is the simple division of Hindu Society to four groups—Brahmin (the Priestly), Kshatriya (The ruler and soldier), Vaisya (Merchant) and Sudra (peasant labourer and servant). The first three classes are twice born Dwijas as they are entitled to wear the sacred thread in a Vedic ritual called Upanayan. The untouchables are mlechhas are out side the above four varnas.

A simple distinction between the caste and varna is to say that caste is based on birth, but varna is associated with action. An uneducated Brahmin enjoys a place of honour by virtue of his birth to an upper caste, where as an educated Sudra remains low in social status because he belongs to a low caste. But the varna system does not attach much importance on birth, but on action. In varna system a Brahmin will be respected only when he teaches to impart knowledge. Teaching is his basic work. The varna puts emphasis on ethical quality and merit of an individual. But in caste, emphasis is laid on birth rights. Caste system is rigid, but varna system is flexible.

It has been claimed that American Negroes comprise a caste. This claim is justified in the sense that many close parallels between social life in traditional India and in modern America can be drawn. Law in many American states forbids inter-racial marriage. The opportunity to enter different spheres of work is either closed or restricted to Negroes. This argument does not find favour among many scholars. They observed that resemblence between traditional India and modern America is more superficial. It is doubtful that such a term as caste properly describes the present social relation between American whites and Negroes.

Scholars have given various definitions of caste. According to Lundera, "a caste is a rigid social class into which members are born."

According to Anderson and Parker, "Caste is that extreme form of social class organization in which the position of individuals in the status hierarchy is determined by descent or birth."

H.H. Risley defines, "caste as a collection of families

or group of families bearing a common name, claiming a common descent from a mythical ancestor, human or divine, professing to follow the same professional calling and who form a single homogenous community."

A.L. Kroeber defines, "caste as an endogamous and hereditary subdivision of an ethnic unit occupying a position of superior or inferior rank or social esteem in comparison with other such subdivision". Green says, "caste is a system of stratification where upward or downward mobility does not occur."

F.G. Bailey says, "A caste is a group of actual or potential kinsmen".

Cooley says, "that when a class is some what hereditary, we may call it a caste."

Blunt says, "caste is an endogamous or collection of endogamous groups, bearing a common name, membership of which is hereditary, imposing on its members certain restriction in the matter of social intercourse, generally forming a single homogenous community".

Karve defines caste, "as an extended kinship group in which every member is either an actual or a potential kin of another".

M.N. Srinivas defines, "caste as a heredity, usually localised group, having a traditional association with an occupational and a particular position in the local hierarchy of castes. Relations between castes are governed among other things by concepts of pollution or purity, and generally, maximum commensality occurs with the caste".

According to Ketkar, "A caste is a group having two characteristics: (1) Membership is confined to those who are born of members and includes all persons so born: (2) The members are forbidden by social law to marry outsides the group.

In some castes there are several hundred sub castes. The sub caste is predominantly endogamous unit. Sub castes are either purely local castes or they constitute associations which are delimited and especially designated according to actual or alleged descent, former or present kind of occupational pursuit or other differences in style of life. They consider themselves as parts of caste and in addition to their own names carry the name of the caste. Thus sub-caste signifies a sub-division of a large caste. In cases where a caste group has split into several smaller endogamous groups, the use of this term for the latter is justified. But where the new group is the result not of the fission but of the fusion of two different groups it would be incorrect to call it a sub caste. Weber holds that today one caste frequently contains several hundreds of sub-castes. In such cases, these sub-castes may be related to one another exactly or almost exactly as are different castes. If this is the case, the sub-castes, in reality, are castes in which the caste name common to all of them has merely a historical significance.

The arrangement of several caste groups in a particular order of relationship in society constitutes the caste system. The groups constituting a caste system are differentiated, interaction and interdependent parts of a larger society. Caste, caste system and casteism all constitute an input of politics in India.

Religious Definition of Caste

The centrality of caste in Indian society and the religious definition of it became a part of the conventional wisdom of comparative sociology, so that social stratification—or of comparative sociology so social hierarchy—was perceived as being essentially a religious phenomenon, emanating some how from the very nature of Hinduism. This became the predominant view of Indian society among those who were specialists on India and also among those who were not.

Nirad Chandra Chaudhury has written bitingly about the "Western legend of Hindu spirituality" and argued that many educated Indians found it convenient to acquiesce in the legend and even to promote it. It gave them a kind of comfort in the face of India's manifest economic and political inferiority to the west to feel that they were spiritually superior. Chaudhury's own erudite work on Hinduism, marked as it is by many angularities, pays very little attention to caste.

Emile Senart, who published an influential book on caste at the end of the nineteenth century, wrote, "Hindu society is regulated by religious custom, and the law books are essentially collections of religious percepts".

Henry Maine, writing in the second half of the nineteenth century, had found it difficult to detach Hindu law from Hindu religion, and the belief became widely established that Hindu society was unchangeable because it was rooted in immutable religious observance.

Max Weber, perhaps the most out-standing comparative sociologist of all time, clearly defined the social identity of the Hindu in terms of caste, and of caste in terms of ritual. He says, "Caste, that is, the ritual rights and duties it gives and imposes, and the position of the Brahmins, is the fundamental institution of Hinduism. Before everything else, without caste there is no Hindu". Even those who would broadly accept this view might point two significant exceptions: (a) Hinduism always had a place for the renounecr and (b) The sannyasi might still be considered a Hindu, although without caste or clan.

Bougle, another sociologist, was an outsider to Indian studies and he had not done field work in India or learnt any of its classical or modern languages. Yet his work on caste has had great influence among scholars. He wrote, "The caste system allows all regimes to pass over its head;

it alone remains". He drew attention repeatedly to the inseparability of caste and Hinduism.

From the above definitions, all observers are agreed that, caste is basically a religious institution and Hinduism is defined more by the observance of caste rules than by fidelity to some precise dogma. The assumption about Hinduism in much of the early sociological writings is that, religion and social structure are inseparable and Hinduism stands not only for a particular religion but also for a particular social structure, that structure being caste. Western writers on religion, including Western sociologists, rarely make such an assumption about Christianity. They see quite clearly that Christianity as a system of beliefs and practices has certain autonomy. Autonomy in the sense that it can be transferred, more or less easily, from one social or historical context to another. Thus, the peculiar feature of Hinduism makes it quite different from Christianity, Islam or Buddhism. This poses an intriguing problem for the sociologist of religion. To be sure, there is every where some relationship between religion and social morphology, but why should the two be inseparable in only one particular case? This assumption of inseparability leads directly to the question whether Hinduism is at all a religion in the true sense of the term.

There is a continued emphasis on the religious basis of caste, so that the system appears to be pervaded by a general aura of ritual and ceremonial. Even when such subjects as endogamy, exogamy, division of labour, occupational specialization, craft practices and so on are being discussed, we are never far away from the world of religion, magic and superstitions. There fore without caste there is no Hinduism.

2

Origin of Caste System in India

Caste system is a special peculiarity of Indian society. The most significant example of a caste system is the one incorporated in Hindu society. Every Hindu necessarily belongs to caste of his parents and in the caste he inevitably remains. No accumulation of wealth and no exercise of talents can alter his caste status and marriage outside his caste is prohibited and severely discouraged. This system is as old as the Aryan culture in India.

The origin date of caste system in India cannot be ascertained. The Indo-Aryan literature is available in the form of Vedas, Upanisadas, Aranyakas and Dharma Sutras throw light on the caste system. The *Rigveda* refers to Arya and Dasa as two types of people. Both the types had differences in complexion, language, religious practices and physical features. The *Rigveda* frequently refers to Brahmins, Kshatriyas, and Vaisayas, but only once to the Sudras. The untouchables or Mlechhas are outside the above four Varnas. In the Purusosukta of *Rigveda* there is reference to four orders of society emanating from the sacrifice of Brahmins. The names of these four orders are given as Brahmin comes from mouth, Kshatriya from the arms and Vaisya from the thigh and Sudra coming from the feet of the creator. The particular limbs associated with these division and the order in which they are mentioned are a sharp distinction between the three higher classes and the Sudras. According to Manu the duty of the Brahmin was to study and teach, to perform sacrifice and to receive gifts. The duty of the Kshatriya was to protect the people. The chief function of Vaisya was to pursue trade and earn money. The Sudra was merely to serve the three higher classes. Each man in the society was given a specific place and work to perform. Thus, the four division of caste was purely functional.

Besides the Sudras, there were some people below the status of above four castes. These included untouchables, oucastes, Chandals, depressed classes etc. They were not admitted into Aryan villages. They had no entry to the temples. The Brahmins were the *Dharma Sutra* writers. They assigned duties and occupation and got it recorded in the Dhramasastras. Whatever the Brahmins said or recorded became the tradition or social rule.

The priest class gradually gained more power and importance. They maintained their superiority by all possible means. They prescribed food for each caste. Thus, caste system got crystallized as social division.

About the origin of this system some scholars say it is the product of culture conflict between the Aryans of the north and Dravidians of the south whom they invaded thousand years ago. Other scholars say it was due to the differences in colour between the lighter invaders and the "darker" native population. The conquerors assigned duties and prescribed food to their subject. Some other scholars say that the division of labour was the basis of Indian Caste System.

It is in India that caste has its complete development. The history of Indian caste system is extremely complex and its causes are manifold. Any attempt to explain the system on the basis of a single factor may therefore, be inadequate and unsound. Religion seems to have deeply influenced Hindu caste structure. Once Hindu religion was adopted it reinforced the stratification on the basis of division of labour.

Abbe Dubors, a European observer regarded caste as an artificial creation. He saw it as a device of cleverer priest class for permanent division and subjection of the masses.

J.H. Hutton did not agree with the view of the Abbe Dubors. He was of the opinion that so deeply rooted and pervasive a social institution as the caste system could hardly have been imposed by an administrative measure.

Sir Herbert Risley and Dr. Ghurye attributed racial differences to the origin of caste. John C Nesfield discussed caste from occupational point of view. Dahlman regarded Indian society as organized originally into three natural groups—the priest, the nobility and the bourgeoise. Each class represented religious, the political and the economic interests of the national life respectively.

There are hundreds of caste groups in India and they are further subdivided. The major castes of Brahmins, Kshatriyas, Vaisyas and Sudras represent only the breast outline of the elaborate caste system. In India presently nearly about 5 000 castes and subcastes are listed. The caste in India in fact is an endogamous kinship group known as 'Jati' linked by marriage and lineage, and for the most part locally identifiable. There are thousands of Jatis in which the social system is organised.

The idea of defilement is common in every caste system and reveals how caste prevents common participation of the various groups in the social life. The rigidity of caste lines permitted very little interaction between different castes. Each lived in segregated residential areas and distinctive marks on the face or special costumes served as a sign of special rank. Whatever may be the other causes, but hereditary occupation was the first step of origin of caste. Every caste maintained their social purity and followed certain customs and traditions. Each caste inculcated a feeling or consciousness about its members. The members of the same caste developed a fellow feeling and spirit of cooperation. Above all it provided a stable social condition to every caste.

Merits and Demerits of Caste System

The caste system has both merits and demerits; since it has survived over several years, therefore it is appropriate to evaluate the system to find out its good and bad aspects.

Merits

The caste system provides a stable social condition. Every individual born in Hindu family has the guarantee of his social status. He is provided with a permanent body of association influencing his birth, education, marriage and profession or calling. The caste takes care of so many things of his life from birth to death. Nothing can be more efficiently managed than the caste system in India.

It provides the spirit of cooperation. The members of the same caste develop a fellow feeling and spirit of cooperation. Between the rich and the poor one can see a sense of equality which is good for the society.

Since caste is based on economic pursuit, no member in the family remains unemployed. Family tradition automatically serves the purpose of economic pursuit and solves unemployment.

Since caste is endogamous there is no marriage outside the caste. That way caste maintains its purity. But, Brahmins and Kshatriyas do not get polluted by marrying in low caste.

Each caste follows certain customs and tradition. With regard to food, dress, social functions and behavior each caste follow its rules. That brings a feeling of equality.

The caste inculcates a feeling or consciousness about its members. Thereby it avoids inner tension and conflict. Inside the caste any fraction is generally not seen. If in politics the members support an ideology and a candidate they give full support. That contributes to the integration of members of the community.

In a society various types of works are to be performed. For example, worship in a temple is considered as dignified and scavenging the street is not considered a dignified work. But caste provides religious sanction to each function. One justifies his function by the doctrine of Karma. That way an unwilling worker also does his job willingly.

Since each caste specializes a particular job in course of time the job becomes a family monopoly. All the technical aspects and secrets about the function are known to the family. The technique and tools are passed by one generation to another, from father to son. That way the society benefited.

Demerits

Caste system being rigid, denies the mobility of members either vertically or horizontally. Once born to a caste there is no escape from the caste restrictions.

Hindu society has often been criticized for the practice of untouchability. It denies social equality. It is against the spirit of humanism. It is humiliating and discriminatory.

The caste system has created social division. The Hindu society had become weaker by this caste system. High and low, or upper and lower is harmful to unity.

Caste system depends upon imposing a profession. But it does not guarantee better performance. Father may be a good artisan, but his son may not be equal or better.

Caste system not only divides the society, it also divides the nation. Division may give rise to discontent. Caste patriotism gets priority over national interest. It creates undesirable situation in national integration.

Caste system prevents level of aspiration to grow, because it has foisted a professional as member. He may not have the urge to fight for better life and progress. Self-contentment is bad. It prevents social progress.

Caste system very often promotes superstitious blind loyalty and total submission. It denies equal rights to men and women. Though caste rules are made by man, they are considered to be divine and infallible. There is no freedom. The principle of democracy is irrelevant to caste system.

3

Caste During Muslim and British Rule

In Hindu society, there were four principal castes (i.e. Brahmins, Kshatriyas, Vaisyas, and Sudras) in order to rank and status and indefinite number of so-called mixed castes of varying status and the despised castes who were placed at the bottom of society. The old position of the Brahmins and Kshatriyas was materially affected by the Muslim conquest of India. The Brahmins lost their royal patronage. They got no job in administration. They lost the opportunity of earning a lot of money by officiating as priests in sacrifices. The new Smritis laid down that they could pursue agriculture through hired labour. Both agriculture and trade were the occupations of the people of all castes. The new commentaries on the Smritis allowed them to give less time to their original occupation and content themselves with the study of Just a part of the Vedas in which they were interested and in some cases with that of the Puranas alone. This was an admission of the decline of the Vedic studies during Sultanate period. There was also a change in the attitude of the Brahmins towards the Sudras.

The Kshatriyas lost not only political power but also the opportunity of earning their livelihood as soldiers, except in Rajasthan, central India and the Himalayan region in the northwest. Guru Nanak had commented on the demoralization of the Kshatriyas in these words— "Kshatriyas have forsaken their religion and adopted the language of the Mlechhas." This comment refers to the acceptance of service by the Kshatriyas under the Muslim rulers and their imitation of Muslim manners and systems. The changed position of the Kshatriyas had a direct impact on Hindu society as a whole.

The Sudras were divided into two categories. Those of the lower category were looked down upon as interior, as the untouchables. The number of mixed castes had gone up to 64 and those were divided into two groups.

Detailed rules were prescribed to avoid contact with the despised castes. Purification by bathing with clothes was prescribed for touching chandals. Different penanceas were to be undertaken by a Brahmin for conversing, or sleeping on the same bed, or going to company with a Chandala, for looking at or touching a Chandala, for drawing water from a tank owned by a Chandala, for drawing water from a well from which water had been drawing a Chandala vessel, for eating the food of a Chandala or living for some times in the same house with the Chandala or for the entrance of a Chandala in the house of a Brahmin etc.

The caste rules and the rules governing the relations between the various castes laid down in the Shastras were not strictly followed. Some Brahmins followed the occupation of the Kshatriyas and some Sudras assumed the Kshatriyas occupation, of ruling and fighting. The common practice was to marry in one's own caste but inter-caste marriages were not unknown.

The Hindu as well as the Muslim society was organized on the basis of the caste system. In case of the Hindus the caste system had been the basis of society since the earliest times. During the Mughal Period also it continued to be the basis of social setup, although its rigorous greatly reduced due to contact with the Muslims which believed in the principles of equality and brotherhood of man. The attitude of exclusiveness which had prevailed amongst the Hindus during the Sultanate period slowly died out because of the better treatment and more economic facilities provided to them by the Mughal rulers. By this time the Hindus had also given up their earlier attitude of keeping aloof from the Muslims whom they designated assimilates. In keeping with the changed situation they began consider the Muslims and the descendants of the Muslims as Indians. Even the Muslims started feeling great attachment for the new land. The Brahmins not only took to the study of the Persian language to acquire high positions under the Government but also took up professions other than their traditional duties.

The caste system of the Hindus also left its impact on the Muslims. During the times of Mughals they were divided into four castes – Sayeed, Sheikh, Mughal and Pathan. The Sayeeds claimed descent from Fatima, daughter of Prophet. The Sheikhs are of pure Arab descent. The Mughals claimed descent from the Mughal race and were sub-divided into Persian and Chugtai. The fourth consisted of Pathan who spoke a distinct language known as Pasto. The existence of the caste system amongst the Muslims has also been acknowledged by their great leader Prof. Mohammad Iqbal. He says "Religious adventurers set up different sects and fraternities ever quarrelling with one another, and there are castes and subcastes like the Hindus, surely we have out-Hindued the Hindu himself, we are suffering from double caste-system, the religious caste system, which we have either learned or inherited from the Hindu".

The advent of the British rule in Indian caused the emergence of a new social classes. It was the direct consequence of the establishment of a new social economy and political administration, a new type of state system, a new type of social system and a stable administrative machinery matching along with the spread of new education.

Massive social transformation took place in the country that had its inevitable effect on the pace of political modernization. Primarily, the new social classes came into existence as a result of the basic economic changes brought about by the constitutional experiments made by the foreign power in order to consolidate the roots of its colonial hold, the penetration of Indian society by commercial and other forces from the outside capitalist world and the establishment of modern industries in India. All this had its manifestation in social as well as political spheres.

The advent of the European merchants and missionaries, their contacts with the people of India coupled with the hold of the British over the political destiny of this country started a process of social change that gathered momentum as time passed and that became more rapid after the conquest of Bengal by the lords of the East India Company. A record of the social and political history of India from 1756 on wards looks like, in the main, a story of the social policy and changes that occurred in the course of about 200 years of British rule, largely as a consequence of western education and commercial progress, of land reforms and legal administration. The old order yielded place to new as a result of which barriers created by caste system became loose, transposition of ranks took place owing to the betterment of the economic lot of the western – educated people; out of the old classes into which Indian society was divided new groups emerged which although differing in wealth, education, profession and occupation, possessed changed characteristics, though these were not as fundamentally different from each other so as to make them socially heterogeneous groupings.

In the first half of the 19th century not only did the British conquerors encourage Christian missionaries, but reform minded Governor–Generals instituted law as against such extreme Hindu practices as Sati, infanticide, and human sacrifice. Percival Spear, a noted historian, explains that liberal Governor-Generals and other officials hoped to acculturate Indians to Western values. The decision was taken to educate an elite through English medium instruction; this was seen by some Indians as a threat to sanskritik and Arabic instruction.

The introduction of western education developed a feeling of suspicion in the minds of conservative sections of the Hindu community. After the introduction of English education, railways, post and telegraphs, the conservative Hindus thought that the British Government would convert India to Christianity. The missionary was to be seen everywhere in the school, in the hospitals, in the prisons and at the market place. The Hindu society apprehended that the British Government would destroy their social polity by legalizing the Religious Disabilities Act of 1856. Lord Dalhousie had passed this Act to enable the Hindu converts to inherit their ancestral property.

Considerable numbers of Brahmin caste members' form Oudh were in the Bengal Army. They were resentful because their princely state, Oudh, was integrated into British India in 1856. Then, there was an enlistment act, which required new recruits to agree to serve overseas—a violation of a Hindu prohibition on overseas travel. During the Crimean War the Indian sepoys were forced to move on the high seas against their will. Lord Canning, the successor of Lord Dalhousie, passed the General Service Enlistment Act in 1856. According to this Act was provided that no sepoy was to be recruited who would refuse to fight across the sea. The soldiers who embraced Christianity were promoted to the higher ranks. With the introduction of the Enfield rifles a rumour began to spread among the sepoys that the cartridges of the rifles were made of the fats of cow and pig. The Hindu and Muslim sepoys thought the Britishers intend to destroy their caste. As Percival Spear, believes that, "Fear of loss of caste" was the main cause of the Mutiny of 1857.

Later on, with the incoming of modern industrial organization and the growth of industrial cities, large numbers of people congregated in cities of mixed population, away from the influence of their homes and unobserved by their caste or village people.

During the early period of British rule the practice of the rulers over the three presidencies was not uniform. While organizing the integrity of caste organization, the Bengal government allowed suits for restoration of caste to be entertained by the ordinary courts. It was held that cases of expulsion from clubs or voluntary associations were of an entirely different nature from excommunication from caste.

In Bombay, however, the pertinent regulation expressly provided that no court shall interfere in any caste question, "beyond of damages on account of the alleged injury to the caste and character of the plaintiff arising of the membership of a caste are held to be wholly with in the jurisdiction of the caste. It is only when a complainant alleges that a legal right either of property or of office is violated by his exclusion from the caste that a suit may be entertained by a court of law. This autonomy of caste, it is further held, exists only under the law and not against it. Hence caste – proceedings must be according to usage, giving reasonable opportunity of explanation to the person concerned and must not be influenced by malice".

The first British administration on the Bombay side employed, as early as, 1826, officials like Borradaile and Steele, to make compilations of the various usages and customs of the many castes of the presidency. These painstaking officers made useful compilations. But similar compendiums were not prepared in other provinces. The result was that the Widow-remarriage Act of 1856 contained clauses practically violating the customs of some of the so-called lower castes. While legalizing the marriage of a

Hindu widow, this Act deprived such a remarried widow of all her rights and interests in her deceased husband's property. Fortunately the courts have taken a reasonable view of these sections of the Act and have decreed that the Act with its restrictive the aid of this Act, remarry according to their caste-usage. Widows of castes allowing remarriage forfeited their rights and interests in their deceased husband's property only when caste-usage enjoined such forfeiture. When any caste council, in utter ignorance of its changed status, ventures to step in as a tribunal to try one of its defaulting members, it is promptly made to realize the force of law. Similarly the Castes-Disabilities Removal Act of 1850 dealt another blow at the integrity of caste. This Act provided that a person does not forfeit his ordinary rights of property by loss of caste or change of religion.

A resolution of the Government of Bombay Finance Department, dated 17th September, 1923, expressly, prohibited recruitment to the lower service from the advanced class of Brahmins and others till a certain proportion of the posts was held by members of the intermediate and backward classes. While inviting applications for vacancies under their charge required the applicant to state his caste and subcaste.

British administrators used caste names as a convenient mode of description of persons. The police reports while giving details about offenders also mention their caste. The Railway risk-note, that every sender of parcels had to fill in and sign, had, at least an entry for the caste of the sender. Perhaps the caste-entry had been inserted to enable the officers concerned to from a rough estimate of the moral character of the person.

The unique institution of caste did not fail to arouse intellectual curiosity among officials as well as no officials in British India. Some of the early officials like Elliot,

Dalton, Shearing and Nesfield evinced their interest in the subject by collecting information and publishing it with their comments. Later on officials, however, adopted the easier method of utilizing the decennial census for collecting and presenting the information and indulging in the theories of the origins of caste. This procedure reached its culmination in the census of 1901 under the guidance of Sir Herbert Risley of ethnographic fame. It may be argued that, if the British masters of India did not take any comprehensive step to minimize the evil effects of caste which they openly deplored, it must be said to their credit that they did not at the utterances of some responsible British officers, after the rising of 1857 was quelled, it is not possible to endorse this view. The rising of 1857 opened the eye of the administrators of the country as well as of the students of British Indian History to the potentialies of caste. It was almost the unanimous opinion of persons connected with the Government of India that the deep causes of the rising were to be found in the fact that the Bengal Army was composed largely of the higher castes, viz. the Brahmins and the Rajputs. The special commission presided over by Lord Peel, which was appointed to suggest a reorganization of the Indian Army, took evidence from many high officials who were sometime or other closely connected with India. Lord Elphinstone opined that it was desirable that man of different castes should be enlisted in the Army, while Major General H.T. Tucker went further and insisted on the necessity of keeping the country under British domination through the policy of dividing and separating into distinct bodies—The nationalities and castes recruited to the Army. The commission recommended that, "The native Indian Army should be composed of different nationalities and castes" Lord Ellenborough advised the same, but clearly pointed out that the recommendation was based solely on the ground of British interests and not on the consideration of efficiency of the Army. He lamented the fact that, if the suggested procedure were adopted, we must abandon the hope of ever again seeing native army composed like that we have lost, It was an army which under a General would have marched victorious. Ever since then the Indian Army has been studiously purged of the higher castes.

The lesson of the rising of the 1857 and the safety of the British domination in India was very closely connected with keeping the Indian people divided on the lines of caste, was driven home to the British rulers. Some officials like Sir Lepel Griffin thought that caste was useful in preventing rebellion, while James Ker, the principal of the Hindu College at Calcutta wrote the following in 1965, "the existence of our role may be doubted."

The maxim of 'divide and rule' began to be preached by historians and journalists alike. Because the rising was largely the work of soldiers of the high caste Brahmins and Rajputs, there was a clamour in England that the high caste sepoys should be exterminated. Suspicion of high castes therefore dates from the Rising.

The movement for freedom lead not only to the intensification of nationalism and the desire for freedom, but also to the rise of Communalism, Casteism, Linguism and Regionalism. The Minto-Morley Reforms of 1909 conceded separate electorates to Muslims, Sikhs, Indian Christians, Anglo-Indians and Europeans. Valentine Chirol, in his book, '*Indian Unrest*' published in 1910, asserted that Brahminism and western education constituted a serious threat to the continuance of the British rule in India. During the World War I, the expectation of transfer of more power to Indians after the war made the non-Brahmin leaders of the composite-Madras presidency to fear that Brahmins will become more powerful. So they wanted that there should be communal representation. There were similar sentiments in Bombay and Bengal presidencies also. This led to the movement becoming political. The non-Brahmin leaders of the old composite state of Madras formed the South Indian Federation in 1916 to advance, and protect the interests of the non-Brahmins. The Federation later on called itself the Justice Party. It started newspapers in English and other languages to educate and put forward the case of the non-Brahmins. In the same way many weeklies were started in the various Indian languages by caste organizations in different parts of India.

The Brahmins monopolized the Post-Graduate classes and the Government jobs in Mysore state. In 1918 the Government appointed Miller-Committee to recommend how the Backward classes could be helped to secure better representation. In its report, the committee recommended that all communities, except the Brahmins, the Europeans and the Anglo-Indians, should be included in the term backward classes.

When the Secretary of State for India, Montague visited India in 1917-18, the Justice Party, representing the Non-Brahmins in the South was outspokenly against the Brahmin community. The Montague-Chelmsford reforms published in July 1918 adopted the Principle of Diarchy. In the Madras state, the Justice Party automatically secured the majority of the seats since the Non-Brahmins constituted about 97 per cent of the population. The Justice Party utilized its political power to apply the principle of reservation for admission to the Post-Graduate and professional courses and for recruitment to the jobs in the Government. The Miller Committee of Mysore State also made similar recommendations.

There were many socio-religious movements which brought many changes in the outlook towards a caste-ridden society. During the Muslim rule the Hindus were confronted with an unexpected crisis due to increasing conservatism and caste rigidity. The Muslim rulers created an unbearable situation for the lower caste people who preferred to leave Hinduism and embrace Islam. Many low caste Hindus in order to avoid social ostracism accepted conversion, because in Islam there was no caste discrimination. The British bought with them a casteless and a literature full of thoughts on individual liberty. As a result Raja Rammohun, Debendranath Tagore started movements which aimed at liberalizing religion and practicing the brotherhood of man. Social inequalities like rigid caste system and untouchability, exploitation and torture of the low caste people had crept into the society. In such a condition Bhakti movement became a new approach to caste system. It assured no caste system, no dominance of Brahmins and equal accessibility.

Raja Rammohun Roy was the first reformer who tried to rid the Hindu society of its glaring weakness. He raised his powerful voice against the caste system. He was the first to point out the evils of untouchability as observed by the caste. In 1828 he founded the Brahmo Samaja. It had not only monotheism to preach but also to establish a brotherhood wherein man shall not be divided from man because of caste. The Bombay Prathana Samaj inspired by the ideals of Brahmo Samaja in Bengal has also thrown caste overboard. In 1875, Swami Dayananda Saraswati founded the Arya Samaj, which has proved a great religious, social and educational movement in India. The doors of Arya Samaj were thrown open to the members of scheduled caste. Swamy Dayananda preached that the fourfold division of the Hindu people should be substituted for the manifold ramifications of contemporary caste. The one important innovation that this school of thought carried in its programme of reconstruction was that even the fourth class of Hindu society, viz. the Sudras could study the Vedas.

The greater popularity of the Arya Samaj; compared with that of the prarthana samaj tried to revive the ancient purity of the Vedic society and this appealed to the traditional sentiment of the people; Secondly, their sincerity of the demonstrated in actual practice and thirdly, its chief center of activity was transferred to the Punjab, where caste has been flexible. The Ramakrishna Movement and the theosophical movement of Annie Besant also significantly contributed towards the end of caste system.

In 1873 Joti Rao Phole or Phule though a man of Mali caste and of comparative little education, started an association of members called the Satyasodhak Samaj with purpose of asserting the worth of man irrespective of caste. He exhorted the non Brahmin caste not to engage any Brahmin priest to conduct their marriage Ritual, which he tried to reduce to a very simple procedure. He had perceived the necessity of educating the calls of people to whom his appeal was directed and had stated primary schools both for boys and girls of the Non-Brahmin castes as early as 1848. Phule revolted against caste system because it denied ordinary human rights to all the members of the Hindu society. In his writings he demanded representation for all classes of Hindus in all the local bodies, the services and the institutions. It was the late Maharaja of Kolhapur who infused new life into the agitation so much so that Montague and Chelmesford, in their Indian Political reforms, had to grant the demands of separate representation.

At the close of the second round table conference, Prime Minister, Mr Ramsay MacDonald gave, what is famously known as, the communal award on August 16, 1932. The scope of award was a limited one, in the sense that it was confined to the seats to be allotted to the various communities in the provincial legislatures. Separate electorate were introduced for Muslims, Sikhs, Indian Christians Anglo- Indian and women. Seven seats were reserved for Marhattas in Bombey out of the general seats. All qualified voters who were not voters either as a

Mohammedan, Sikhs, Indian Christians Anglo- Indian or European were entitled to vote in the general constituencies. Members of the depressed classes qualified to vote were given the right to vote in the general constituencies. Apart from this, a specific number of seats was assigned to them, to be filled by election from special constituencies in which only members of the Depressed classes, electorally qualified, were entitled to vote. Thus the depressed class voters were given two vote each one in a general constituency and the other in the above-mentioned special constituencies. This was done in view of backward position of the community and to give it an adequate representation. The special constituencies were intended to be reformed in selected areas, where the depressed classes were most numerous. Except in Madras, these constituencies were not to cover the wholly area of a province. In Bengal, because the depressed class voters were in a majority even in some general constituencies, special constituencies were not provided for them, for the time being. Not less than 10% seats were to given to the depressed classes in the Bengal Legislature. It was declared that the special depressed class constituencies would come to an end after twenty years. The net result of this arrangement regarding the depressed classes was that they were accorded separate electorate apart from the caste Hindus, which was a serious innovation.

Mahatma Gandhi had already told the British Government that he would, if necessary, resist, with the very life, any attempt on the part of the British Government to introduce separate electorates for the Depressed classes. He opposed it bitterly because in his opinion that would disrupt the Hindu society and perpetuate untouchability. At the time of the publication of the Award, Mahatma Gandhi was in jail. On September 20,1932 he commenced his fast, unto death to get the wrong righted. But very soon leaders like Pandit Madan Mohan Malviya, C.

Rajgopalchari, Dr Rajendra Prasad, Dr Ambedkar and M.C. Rajah conferred together at Poona for about six days to save the life of Mahatma Gandhi. As a result of these deliberations, the Poona Pact retained joint electorates for the scheduled castes along with the Hindus. But 148 seats were reserved for the Harijans in the provincial legislatures as against 71 seats given to them by the Communal Award. All the members of the Depressed Classes registered in the General Electoral Roll in a constituency were to form an electoral college, which was to elect a panel of four candidates belonging to the Depressed Classes for each of such reserved seats, by the method of single transferable vote. The four persons getting the highest number of vote in such primary election were to be candidates for election by the general electorate. This method was to be followed in the case of seats both in the provincial and in the central legislature, 18% of the seats allotted to the general electorate for the British India in the central legislatures were to be reserved for the Depressed classes. Thus, more than double the seats were given to the Harijans by the Poona Pact than the number allotted to them by the Communal Award.

In 1932 the Harijan Sevak Sangh was formed and the conference at Bombay pledged that the right to use the public roads, wells etc. would be given statutory recognition when the Swaraj Parliament met, in case such a legislation was not passed earlier.

This pledge was reiterated by Gandhi in December 1932 when he expressed, " There could be no rest, there fore for me or for those who by word of mouth or show of hand, willingly endorsed the resolution, until untouchability becomes a thing of the past".

However, Ambedkar warned his followers not to get lost in the temple entry and inter-dinning. He wanted them to solve their economic problems because the temple entry would not give them economic security. In his letter to Thakkar Bapa he said, "the salvation of the depressed class will come only when the caste Hindu is made to think and is forced to feel that he must alter his ways. I want a revolution in the mentality of the caste Hindus." He asserted that such a social revolution will come only when the anti-untouchability league, of which Thakkar Bapa was the joint secretary, launched a campaign all over the country to secure for the depressed classes enjoyment of their civil right such as taking water from the village wells, admission of the children in village schools, etc. How ever, such a civil Campaign, according to Ambedkar, needed an army of workers in the rural parts.

The British rule in India had opened up alternative set of opportunities for status mobility in the caste hierarchy. These opportunities provided the scope for different social groups to take the advantage of them. The introduction of western education, opening of railways, telegraph, postal, flow of information, expansion of internal market, introduction of modern technology, expansion of transport network, and rapid growth of urbanization and industrialisation during British rule in India provided scope to different castes for improving their social status. These changes in the socioeconomic life made the non-privileged castes conscious of their low status. They were disatisfied with the existing social order. This consciousness resulted in an urge for improving their status in the social hierarchy. This was manifested in assuming names other than those by which they were commonly known and getting such claims accepted by the Government as well as society. Different Caste Associations were formed to effectively fight for these claims in an organized way. The lower castes, which have become prosperous or powerful or educated, became assertive in claiming a higher place in the social hierarchy. These changes facilitated social mobility among castes. The British rule, thus, produced radical and lasting changes in Indian society and culture.

Caste and Sanskritisation

It was M.N. Srinivas, the sociologist who first spoke of Sanskritisation. It has been affecting an increasing number of people during and after the British rule. Independence of India in 1947 appears to have quickened the process of westernization. Their bearing on caste system is another aspect, which cannot be ignored.

Although Sanskritisation is an age old process it is an ongoing process of social change in India. It is the process by which a low Hindu caste, changes its customs, ritual, ideology and way of life in the direction of a high caste. Generally, such changes are followed by a claim to a higher position in the caste hierarchy than that traditionally conceded to the claimant caste by the local community. It results only positional changes, not structural. However, it involves mobility by the upward movement of a caste. Thus Sankritisation is a cultural process. The process of change is determined by the dominant caste.

The process of Sanskritisation does not leave the dominant caste free from change. As a major process of social change it has not left any caste untouched. It has also percolated to every corner of the land. There may have been some variation in its degree of intensity and the area, but it has traveled to every part of the country making the process of change universal. The caste system has confronted with the process of Sanskritisation more boldly because caste is a closed system of the society. Wherever Saskritisation has percolated to a jati the changes appear to be in the form of upward movement.

The process of Sanskritisation has been speeded up by rapid change in material culture, viz, industrialization, education, technological progress, literacy and facilities in transport system. The introduction of parliamentary democracy and universal suffrage have helped the growth of Saskritisation. All on a sudden power and position came within the reach of low caste or depressed class people who did not hesitate to claim a new superior social status. But what is possible is only a slight shift within the Varna. The Sudra continues to be a sudra but because he has adopted vegetarianism etc., he may move up slightly in the scale of Jatis within the given varna. As Srinivas himself points out the varna hierarchy "is clear and immutable " It is evident, therefore, that Saskritisation reinforces and consolidates the 'immutable varna hierarchy' rather than dislodge it or modify it. Srinivas further notes "The ordering of the different varna is clearly intended to support the theory of Brahminical Supremacy". As a result, the slight improvement in social position through Saskritisation is severely limited since the Jati as a hereditary endogamous group, continues to occupy the same position in the varna hierarchy. Thus, Saskritisation is not a process by which structural changes in the Hindu society can become possible, it is certainly not the means by which any social change in India can be brought about.

Caste and Westernization

Srinivas has also used the term ' Westernization ' to indicate change in caste system which took place in India during the British rule in the nineteenth and early twentieth centuries. Chiefly westernization implies changes in dress, diet, style of eating, manners etc. The most important change was in the medium of instruction. Westernization started having its impact on the elite because they studied secular subjects with English as the medium of instruction. Another big change introduced in the Indian society by the new system of education is that the schools were thrown open to all people, in contrast to the traditional schools which were restricted to upper – caste children and which transmitted mostly traditional knowledge. However, the children of the lower caste groups did not utilize this facility. This remains even today a formidable problem after nearly three decades since Independence and after nearly a century and a half since the introduction of the new system of education. The reluctance of the lower castes then, a new, is due to the fact that they are content with the caste occupations, however inadequate the income from them may be and however low the resulting social status may be.

Western education also resulted in a big change in the outlook of those educated. Exposure to English literature, history and political institutions made them adopt a humanitarian outlook and promoted in them an active concern for the welfare of all human beings irrespective of caste, creed and other considerations. It promoted equalitarianism and secularism. While traditional education promoted uncritical acceptance of ancient works, western education promoted rationalism and a critical outlook towards events and problems.

While sanskritization process promoted the ' Sacred ' out look, Westernization process promoted the ' Secular ' out look. Here again the conflict has been removed by the constitution which is secular in outlook and emphasis, though the sacred out look continues to be dominant among the elite as well as the masses.

As Srinivas writes, "the Brahmins looked up to the British, and the rest of the people looked up to both the Brahmins and the British. The fact that some of the values and customs of the British were opposed to some Brahminical values made the situation confusing". In spite of these contradictions between Brahmins and Westernism, a section of the Brahmins adopted Westernism because of the prestige of the ways of the masters, and the monetary benefits of secure careers in the Government and commercial offices.

The main concern of the lower castes was to catch up with the Westernized Brahmin who were well educated and who were enjoying the prestige, power and wealth of the Government office. They soon realized that more

"Sanskritization was not enough", since this process only helped them to improve their status with in the "immutable" Varna system. They realized, on the other hand, that the adoption of the Westernization process which helped them to move up in the social scale without the limitations of Jati and Varna. Srinivas has rightly observed, "They thus became more determined to obtain western education and the fruits that only it could yield. High caste dominance in education and in the new occupations thus provided the 'raison d'etre' for the backward classes movement. It is no accident that the movement was the strongest in peninsular India where only one caste the Brahmins, enjoyed a preponderance in higher education, the professions, and the Government employment." The lower castes thus chose Westernization, that is, education through English medium, rather than Sanskritization, as the means to enable them to more up in status in the society.

The scheduled castes politics is also, in a way, the legacy of the British rule in India. During the British rule, India's Harijans and tribes were officially singled out as deserving remedial treatment. The communities were listed on 'schedule' and thus came to be known as 'scheduled castes' and 'Scheduled tribes'. Our British rulers, in their efforts to dismember the Hindu community, also provided for various benefits and reservation of seats for these classes. What began during the British rule did not end with the British rule. The scheduled castes and tribes are even now entitled to special representation and benefits. The competitiveness of electoral politics has added new-dimensions to their original political importance. No political leader, not even the prime minister, can afford to be indifferent to their interests so long as they continue to occupy a strategic position as 'vote bank'. Hence there has been a continuous pressure for policies more oriented to the needs of these castes.

4

Casteism in Free India

India is caste-ridden society. The predominant feature of her social structure is caste system. The introduction of the democratic system and universal adult franchise has given new vigour to the caste system in the post-independence period. As the democratic Government rest on popular values, the different political parties try to pursue different social groups to vote for them. The multi party system and the absence of ideological or class based parties in the country, have also contributed to the importance of caste as a factor. The illiterate people of India who do not understand politics in terms of ideological interests are moved in the name of caste sentiments by various political parties. Caste considerations are always given great importance at the time of distributing the tickets for various positions or forming ministers. It is natural that the people of the same caste group vote for a candidate of their own caste. However, if a candidate of their caste is not available they vote according to the direction of their caste leaders.

Thus, the caste factor continues to be a major factor of electoral parties in free India. All political parties give great weightage to the caste factor in selecting their candidate, in allocating constituencies to their candidates and in canvassing support for their nominees in the election.

In the election campaign, votes are demanded in the names of caste. Caste groups are trapped for committed support. No one can disagree with N.D. Palmer when he observed that "caste considerations are given great weight in the selection of candidates and in the appeals to voters during election campaigns. In elections, castes act as the most important political party. It also plays a basic role in the decision making process. Even the issue of re-organization of states is handled with an eye upon the prevention of undue predominance of a caste group in a particular territory. The party in power tries to use its decision making power to win the favour of major caste groups. Regional political parties, whenever these get the chance to rule their respective states always use political power for furthering the interest of the caste groups which support or can support their regime. Recruitment to political offices is mostly done with due considerations for the caste of the persons. The caste factor always acts as a determinant of people's voting behaviour, their political participation, the party structure and even the governmental decision making. M.N. Srinivas has rightly said, "The caste is so tactly and so completely accepted by all including the most vocal in condemning it that it is everywhere the unit of social action". He further writes, "there is a widespread impression among educated Indians that caste is on its last legs and that the educated urbanized and westernized members of the upper classes have already escaped its bond. Both these does not mean that they have escaped the bonds of caste entirely. The show caste attitude in surprising contexts".

Caste also influences the process of leadership recruitment. In the Indian rural context, caste has been a plank of mobilization, a channel of communication, representation and leadership and a linkage between the electorate and the political process. The role of caste in the working of Panchayat Raj and other institutions of local government has been a recognized reality. We can go to the extent of recording that caste based factionalism in rural areas of India has been one of the most major hindering factor in the organisation and effective working of panchayat Raj and urban local institutions.

Again, under the impact of modern politics, associations of caste have become the hall-mark of political mobilization. They have emerged with the object of pursuing political power, social status and economic interest. Members of Certain caste groups, who were considered low or the lowest in socio-economic hierarchy a few decades ago, now federate to gather into a common organization and then press for their demands. They have gained new confidence and status. They not only actively participate in the political process but also assert their identity and even strive for positions. Thus, politics has become important for the caste and caste for politics in free India.

It is unfortunate that in free India the persecution of lower caste groups by members of some of the upper and middle castes seems to have intensified and is some regions this oppression has taken a sharply violent form. Members of untouchable communities seeking a better economic and social deal have been subjected to harrasment, beating, burning of homes and even murder. The reasons for this unhappy state of affairs are not far to seek. Land ownership in India has not been greatly affected by four decades of legislation except for remedy of the worst abuses of land tenure system left by the British. Hence tensions based on land ownership and occupational advantages express themselves in political conflict. B.K. Nehru, in his Indira memorial lectures at the Kerala University rightly observed, "the atrocities committed on Harijans and other low caste people in many parts of the country and the occasional retaliation of the lower castes against the upper castes is not based on claims of superiority or inferiority of caste; the cause is simple-one caste group possesses land; the other is landless. In the same way, agitations against the increased reservations for backward castes have nothing to do with caste superiority or inferiority; they are clearly motivated by survival. The divisive factor of caste comes into play because on no other basis can those without employment get it; as those who have it naturally refuse to give it up. For the poor and the landless non-Brahmins in some states, the concessions, to which scheduled castes are entitled by law, are a thorn in the flesh. For the landowners of the dominant castes, the rising demands of the lower castes and tenants are a threat to their social and economic position. Besides there is enough evidence to show that in the changed circumstances, younger people of the low castes are not ready to behave in the same docile way in which older people behave. They do not feel committed to the perpetuation of the traditional and social arrangements between castes. When this spirit of challenge confronts the entrenched interests of the dominant caste, the result is often a measure of violence even. Obviously, it means that because of the intolerance of upper castes and the rising aspirations of lower castes, the Indian road to equality is going to be marked by bloody clashes between different castes, though caste may to some analysts appear to be a false category unlike class. The traditional differences between higher and lower castes have acquired a new vigour and have turned, at times, into a violent and fierce struggle for power in society. Thus the growing terrorization of the lower castes by the higher or even intermediary castes, has been becoming a part of rural India's political reality.

Morris Jones found that, "in free India, politics is more important to castes and castes are more important to politics than before. He claims that the top leaders may proclaim the goal of a casteless society, but the newly enfranchised rural masses know only of the language of traditional politics which largely turns about caste. Behind the formal lift of party candidates nominated for the contest, there is probably an inside story of careful calculation in terms of caste appeal".

However, there are indications that dominant castes are becoming less dominant in the Indian villages. They have been forced by the circumstances to make many vital concessions in terms of social vertical mobility. There is also a change in their style of behaviour towards lower castes who, on the strength of théir member and political consciousness, are becoming increasingly confident and ambitious. The enhanced social status has enabled the lower castes to function in the political area as well. Their participation in the Panchayatraj institutions, has now become more meaningful and effective.

After Independence, the national leaders took up the task of framing the constitution. While making constitution they were inspired by the concepts of equality and social Justice. So our constitution made special provisions for the advancement of the scheduled castes and scheduled tribes. The southern states with long history of backward caste movements took lead in the matter. They made special provisions for Other Backward Castes in respect of reservations for them. The reservations for scheduled and scheduled tribes were supposed to be abolished after 10 year. But such is our system that they still continues after 55 years and so far as one can foresee, have become a permanent and unalterable feature of the constitution.

The caste system in free India had experienced many changes because of the changing socio-economic forces. The birth rate of the various castes in India fluctuated from time to time and so did their occupational skills. Hence it paved the way for greater mobility in the context of social stratification. As a result of which various castes and sub-castes were grouped and regrouped.

The western education, modern democratic conceptions, conceptions of equality, social justice, the empirical and scientific outlook and the dynamics of a developing economy, all demanded flexibility in the caste mobility. Highly important activities in the social life seem to be open to both members of all caste groups. Moreover, changing economic and technological conditions, without disturbing the basic caste structure itself, has necessitated shifts in occupation. A differentiation of function, that have placed some high-caste Brahmins in almost all occupations from becoming priests, physicians and even holding jobs in government and private organization. Likewise some low caste people have become scholars and priests. In the post-independence period there have been many attempts to break the hold of the caste system. Constitution of India brought about a radical change by instituting a new principle of Justice which emphasized that all men are equal before the eyes of law. There have been legislative measures to outlaw untouchability and granting equality regardless of caste considerations.

In the changed scenario the caste comes to play a different role. It has its manifestations in the formation of pressure groups and political parties in free India. The caste groups acquire new dimensions and become highly competitive. This resulted in steady politicization of caste groups. The cleavage between different caste groups resulted in social tensions. The upper castes tried to become effective in the political arena. On the other hand the non-privileged caste groups have sought avenues of upward social mobility. Their numerical strength provided them the opportunity to have a sway in politics. The low caste sought to capture the lever of power through political process. The earlier belief that political power was the preserve of the upper castes received a severe jolt. The backward caste people at grass-roots found ample scope to consolidate their dominance in the rural areas in the wake of the socio-economic transformation.

The caste consciousness in free India operating at two contradictory levels: One that every one speaks of transforming a caste ridden society and claims to be in favour of it; secondly, that caste consciousness and solidarity have rapidly increased after that caste system has confronted the new opportunity in the changed economic and political structure.

According to Paul Colenda, six important changes have taken place in India since independence: (i) The establishment of universal adult franchise. (ii) The legal outlawing of untouchability and policy of compensatory discrimination. (iii) The exposition of educational facility and multiplication in the number of people attending schools and colleges. (iv) The increase in white-collar jobs such as teacher and Government officials. (v) The tremendous expansion of the infrastructure in Indian society—buses, road, railways, airways. (vi) Great increase in the productivity of grain. All these changes have had substantial effect on the rural caste politics. To put in other words modernization has sharpened inherited social identities.

5

Movement Against Caste System in India

Just as the caste system has been in India from times immemorial, attempts to abolish has been in India from time immemorial. Swami Vivekananda wrote, "The caste system is opposed to the religion of the Vedanta. Caste is a great custom and all our great preachers have tried to break it down. From Buddhism downwards every sect has preached against caste and every time it has reverted the chains."

Thus right from the times of *Upanishads,* thinkers have spoken against caste system. Buddha preached against the caste system 2,500 years back. The Hindu religion with its caste system and social hierarchy became the order of the day. It heralded the supremacy of the Brahmins over the social and religious order. They dominated over the scenario. They formulated religious rules to support the system. Against this system there were murmurings of protest. It began from the ruling caste of Kshatriyas. Because next to Brahmins, the Kshatriyas were socially prominent and natural leaders of the society. They had the moral strength to challenge the oppressive caste system. Such challenge appeared in the form of two religious movements called Jainism and Buddhism. Both the religions were called protest movements. During the 12th century, Basaveswara developed a new sect which did not admit the caste system. At about the same period, Ramanuja brought a great reform in Vaishnavism. He refused to accept the caste system and welcomed the low caste sudras to enter the temples. The way he repudiated the caste system made him a social reformer. He allowed the sudras to his sect. Ramananda also opposed to caste system and had free social relation with people of low caste. He welcomed all castes to his sect. Among his faithful disciples were Rai Das the cobbler, Sain Das, the barber and Kabir, one Muslim weaver. Right through there have been attempts by great reformer like Kabir to uplift the people belonging to lower castes and to the untouchable caste. Another great saint of the Bhakti cult Chaitanya also denounced caste and proclaimed the universal brotherhood of men. A follower of Chaitanya was above the caste system. Guru Nanaka also opposed to the priestly class and the caste system. Thus, Bhakti cult assured no caste system, no dominance of the Brahmins and equal accessibility.

In the nineteenth century, there were four great movements with the main aim, among other things, to abolish the caste system. Rammohun Roy established the Brahmo Samaj so that people of all castes could gather together and hear discourses from the Upanishads. As Sitanath puts it, "though Rammohun Roy was in favour of social reform and spoke against caste system his writings show that he desired anything more than the removal of the evil customs connected with caste". It was Keshabchandra Sen who along with his friends took practical steps in 1862 of celebrating, though privately, and intercaste marriage". "It was only from 1864 onwards", as Shivanath Shastri writes, "That missionaries were appointed by the Brahmo Samaj who were enjoyed to discard idolatory and caste for they are abomination."

Another great movement against the caste system was the Arya Samaj movement. As Lala Lajpat Rai writes, "The Arya Samaj repudiates caste by birth. It condemns numerous sub-divisions into which Hindu society has been split up by reason of castes and sub-castes. It considers the artificial barrier which caste in India has created to divide men from their fellowmen as pernicious and harmful".

Another movement against the caste system was the Ramakrishna movement. Swami Vivekananda wrote about the degeneration in the religion which discusses whether he should drink a glass of water with the right hand or left and the number of times the hand should be washed to overcome the pollution; he looked upon Hindus as don't – touchists" and Hinduism as the "religion of the Kitchen and of the cooking pot".

The Theosophical movement which established its headquarters at Adyar, Madras, in 1882 was another movement which worked for the abolition of caste system, particularly since 1893, when Annie Besant became the president of the society.

The British brought about a revolution by instituting a new principle of justice, namely 'that all men are equal before law and that the nature of the wrong is not affected by the caste, the person committing it or against when it was committed, by the introduction of the Indian Penal Code in 1860. Even earlier in 1833, the British declared that no person on account of "his religion, place of birth, descent, colour" would be disabled from holding any office or employment. The same principle equality before law and for office in government formed part of the Queen Victoria's Proclamation of 1858. Thus, as for as employment in government and cases in courts of law were concerned, there was no disability for an individual on the ground of his caste. However, right up to the beginning of the present century, the educational opportunities that were provided by the British were largely taken advantage of only by the members of the upper castes, though education was open to people of all castes and creeds. Besides the legal and educational reform, the introduction of the new large-scale industries, which threw open employment opportunities to people of all castes, was another important trend. It may be said that these trends of the nineteenth century were to a large extent responsible for the emergence of some organized movement among the lower castes in the latter part of the nineteenth century and in the beginning of the twentieth century.

One of the earliest organized protest movements among the lower castes was due to the efforts of Jyoti Rao Phule of Poona. He had started primary schools for boys and girls of the non-Brahmin Castes as early as 1848. In 1851, he started an association called the Satya Sodhak Samaj in order to assert the worth of man irrespective of caste. He exhorted the non-Brahmin castes not to engage any Brahmin priest to conduct their marriage ritual. He tried to simplify these procedures.

Another very important attempt of the non-Brahmins was in Madras. The south Indian Liberal Federation (SILF) was formed in 1916 to advance, safeguard, and protect the interests of the non-Brahmin communities. The federation, later known as the Justice Party, also started newspapers in English and Tamil. Actually this was an elite conflict and there was no mass movement behind it. The non-Brahmin elite found that the Brahmin elite, because of their education, was able to capture office of power in Government and so started this movement in order to capture the power from the hands of the Brahmin elite.

Both the Maharashtrian movement and the Madras Movement were eager to get communal representation at the political level, and at the schools and colleges in the educational level and finally, the representation in the recruitment to government offices.

Another movement which arose among the Harijans against the caste system was Sri Narayan Guru's movement in Kerala. Sri Narayan Guru a leader of the Izhavas, an untouchable group of Kerala, had a revolt against the caste system.

Narayana Guru was born in 1854 in a small village called Chempazhanthi on the outskirts of Trivandrum City, of small peasant stock. He had no modern English education. That marks him out from the other social reformers of the latter half of the nineteenth century. But he had a good education in the traditional manner, learning Tamil and Sanskrit in both of which he became very proficient. Although married very early in accordance with his parents wishes he never cohabited with his wife and was a life long celibate (Brahmachary).He left her soon after marriage and wandered forth into the wide world, just as Buddha did. For some time nobody knew where he was. It is believed that he traveled extensively in Tamilnadu and spent much time wandering in the forests, meditating in mountain caves and mixing with all sorts of people irrespective of caste and religion. He chose as his life's mission the crusade against the caste system and the uplift of his fellowmen. Although he claimed to be a follower of Sankara, he was an uncompromising opponent of the caste system.

After returning from the life of a wanderer he settled in Aruvipuram in Trivandrum district, a beautiful site on the bank of the Nayyar river. There on the Sivarathri day of 1888 he struck the first great blow against caste by installing a Sivalinga picked up from the river-bed and establishing a temple. When asked what right he, a non-Brahmin and a low caste person at that, had to install the idol of Siva, he coolly answered: "It is an Ezhava Siva that I have installed."

The first campaign that the Guru undertook was to establish temples for the Ezhavas wherever they wanted them. The purpose of this campaign was two-fold, First, to wean away the Ezhava community from the worship of local tribal Gods with animal sacrifices and other uncivilized rites and teach them to worship Hindu Gods in the way high-caste Hindus did, thereby asserting a sort of equality with caste-conscious Hindus. Ezhavas themselves performed the pooja in these temples after getting trained for the same in their own temple schools.

However appealing this programme might have been to the sense of self-respect of the Ezhava community, this alone could never hope to end the evil of caste system. For that a frontal assault on the citadels of caste was necessary. Ezhavas could enter freely the temples established by the community, but they could not use the roads by the side of the caste Hindu temples. So, that right had to be asserted. And for that either a royal proclamation or legislation was necessary. This was the aim of the famous Vaikom satyagraha. This was still far away that is, in 1924. Before that a lot of things happened not only in the Ezhava community, but also in the Nair and other communities.

Among the Ezhavas the most important event that took place was the foundation of the Sree Narayana Dharma Paripalana Yogaam (SNDP Yogam) in 1903 at Aruvipuram. The first Secretary of the Yogam was Kumaran Asan, who worked for about 19 years in that capacity. It worked for the removal of the disabilities of the Ezhavas, including the disability of untouchability. Many educated young men began to join the Yogam.

More than any other organisation, it was the Indian National Congress itself which had become radicalized by the emergence of the leadership of Mahatma Gandhi in 1919, followed by the non-cooperation movement that gave a fillip to the anti untouchability movement. T.K. Madhavan, a follower of Narayana Guru and an Ezhava by caste, was an ardent Congressman. He went as a delegate to the session of the Indian National Congress at Kakinada in 1923, met Congress President and other leaders and got passed a resolution recommending starting of a movement for the abolition of untouchability to be launched under Congress auspices. Armed with the resolution, Madhavan returned to Kerala and persuaded the Kerala Pradesh Congress Committee (KPCC) to launch a Satyagraha for the right of the untouchables to use the roads running by the side of the Mahadev Temple at Vaikom. This Satyagraha electrified the entire country. But it did not succeeded fully in the limited objective of gaining free use of the road by all including the untouchables. It needs to be remembered however that twelve years later that is in 1936, all Hindu temples and not only the roads were thrown open to all Hindus by Royal Proclamation in Travancore. There is no doubt that the Vaikom satyagraha paved the way for the abolition of untouchability ultimately.

The Vaikom satyagraha is important not only for the role played by the untouchable communities but even more so for the role played by the caste Hindu Communities and especially the Nairs. The Nair community as a whole was sympathetic to the satyagraha. A Savarna (caste Hindu) jatha led by the famous Mannath Padmanabhan, who at that time was a young firebrand, marched on foot from Vaikom right upto Trivandram and presented a memorandum to the Maharani Regent urging that all public roads in the State including those touching temples be opened to people of all castes and creeds including the untouchables.

The same is the case with Guruvayoor Temple entry Satyagraha which was started on November 1, 1931 during the time when Gandhiji was in London attending the Second Round Table Conference. The satyagraha assumed the form of volunteers standing outside the temple gopuram at a distance upto which untouchables were allowed to come and shouting slogans and chanting Bhajans. This went on day after day for several months. When this proved futile the renowned Congress leader K. Kelappan began a hunger strike before the temple on September 1, 1932, the very same day that Gandhiji began his fast in Poona in protest against the British Government's communal award after returning from the round table conference. Kelappan ended his fast on the advice of Gandhiji conveyed through a telegram from Yervada prison in which Gandhiji had been lodged and undertaken his fast to pledge his support to the cause of temple entry and abolition of ineducability. This pledge could be ultimately redeemed only after Congress came to power in Madras Provinces in 1946 and legislation for Temple entry was enacted.

Thus the movement for the abolition of untouchability was a truly National Movement in Kerala and it churned up the entire people during the early decades of the 20th century. Although Nambudiris were the highest caste in Kerala, they also had peculiar problems of their own. It was the custom that only the eldest male heir of the Nambudiri family could marry in his own caste. The junior members were to be content with marrying women of the Nair or other communities, which were, supposed to be inferior to Nambudiris. This was a device intended to keep the family wealth intact and not fritter it away by partition. The young man of the Nambudiris Community, touched by the unhappy fate of their sisters, started a movement of reform which included such aims as the right of every male members to marry in his own caste, the abolition of polygamy, widow remarriage, education of the girls and the right to individual partition of family property. They built up a powerful organisation called the Nambudiris Yogakshema Sabha which was found in 1908 and later the Nambudiris young men's organisation which was much more militant. It organized picketing of old men's marriages and collected money from house to house for educating girls. Comrade E.M.S. Namboodiripad was one of the leaders of this movement before he took to active Congress politics. Ultimately their agitation was crowned with success and all the aims for which they fought were attained.

While on the subject of missionaries one can not afford to forget the inspiration imparted by them to the agitation for the right to cover their breasts by the Nadar women in south Travancore. In the old days, women belonging to the lower castes couldn't cover theirs breasts. When Christian Missionaries started their work among the Nadars in South Travancore and converted many of them to Christianity they encouraged the Nadar women to cover their breasts with blouses or Kuppayam. This was resented by upper castes like Nairs who began to beat up such women. The Nadar young men choose to retaliate a riot ensued. The missionaries took up cause of the Nadars with the Governor of Madras who intervened and ultimately the Maharaja of Travancore was forced to issue an order permitting Nadar women to cover their breast.

To conclude the distinctive features of the renaissance movement in Kerala may be summed up as follows.

First, the movement was initiated not by a man with modern Western education, but one educated in the traditional way, a Sanyasin.

Secondly, the central point of onslaught was the caste system and all that it signified.

Thirdly, the main force of the movement was the two biggest communities of Kerala, the Ezhavas and the Nairs, one an untouchable community and the other a caste Hindu community.

Fourthly, although it began as social reform movement, later on it merged with and formed a part of the movement for National freedom, under the leadership of the Indian National Congress.

Lastly, western Christian Missionaries working in Kerala also made a contribution to the movement.

A. Ayyappan, in his book "Social Revolution in a Kerala

Village" writes that, C.P. Ramaswamy Iyer, the Dewan of the Travancore state, felt the need for consolidating the Hindus and building up the unity of the Hindus of the state as a counter poise against the growing power and influence of the Christians. The most discontented and at the same time the best organized among the Hindus Caste were the Iravas. Nothing was dearer to the Iravas of that generation than temple entry."

However, in recent years a new class trend has emerged among the Ezhavas. The middle class of this group supported the Congress party, and their leader, R. Shanker, spearheaded the liberation struggle with Manmath Padmanavan of Nayar Service Society and caused the first communist Government in Kerala to be dislodged in 1958. Shankar himself became the Deputy Chief Minister in 1962 and the Chief Minister of Kerala state in 1964. However, the lower classes among the Ezhavas were giving their solid support to the communist party. As V.K.S. Nayar in his article "Communal Interest groups in Kerala" writes, "The SNDP Yogam (an organization established by Narayan Guru in 1902) represents the Ezhava middle class. The vast majority of the Ezhavas have favoured the communist party. Thus there is a gulf between the Ezhava middle-class and the Ezhava lower class".

Agitation was also set up by Ambedkar to remove untouchability. Ambedkar stayed in America for three years and took his Master' Degree and a Doctorate in Economics and returned to India in 1917 when the Franchise Committee was preparing its report for Montague, the secretary and Chelmsford the Viceroy. He met the Franchise Committee and made a strong plea for direct representation of the depressed class in the Bombay legislature in proportion to their population through a separate electorate.

He was a great leader of the Mahar community in Maharashtra to which he belonged and he took many steps to reform the way of life of these people. He urged them to stop the dragging of dead cattle out of the village. He wanted them to become literates and send their children to schools. Finally, he wanted them to dress well and have self respect for themselves. Thus, one of his chief aims was to bring about a revolution in the way of life of the untouchables and in their aspirations for themselves and for their children. On a few occasion Ambedkar made many attempts to forcibly enter the Hindu temple. The right to participate in the public Ganapati festival was secured at least on one occasion. Ambedkar and his followers donned the sacred thread-symbolizing rebirth. The abortive attempt to enter the temple at Amaravati was followed in 1930 by large scale Satyagraha at the Kalaram temple in Nasik. Ambedkar himself disbelieved idol worship. So the programme of temple entry was more for social than for religious purposes. Thus, it looks as if in the period 1920-1930 he was in favour of the temple entry programme in order to establish the rights of the untouchables. But after 1930 he gave up these attempts and concentrated his attention on the improvement of the educational standard of the community and their political status. At the first round table conference he emphasized that untouchables constitute a distinct group and can not be looked upon as the members of the Hindu community. So he wanted a separate electorate to be established for the untouchables.

In May 1920, an All India conference of the untouchables was arranged at Nagapur. It was presided over by the Maharaja of Kolhapur. At the end of this conference Ambedkar made an attempt to consolidate the forces of the depressed classes, by arranging an intercaste dinner. Among the Mahars alone, the community to which Ambedkar belonged, there were 18 sub-castes without interdining and inter-marriage. Ambedkar found that it was very difficult to get the various sub-castes of the Mahars and the sub-castes of the other castes of the depressed classes to join together at a dinner. Thus Ambedkar was faced with two problems; to consolidate all the depressed classes as one group and to get all the Hindus, the Savarn, and the Avarna together so that the Avarna Hindu have their rightful place in the Hindu society.

The great movement started by Mahatma Gandhi was not only against the removal of untouchability, but also against the caste system itself. In 1920, Gandhi wrote: "Untouchability can not be given a secondary place in the programme. Without the removal of the taint, Swaraj is a meaning less term." Thus from 1920 onwards, the Indian National Congress under the leadership of Mahatma Gandhi became committed to the removal of untouchability. In December 1932, the congress at its session in Ahmedabad resolved to start a voluntary organization throughout the country and signed a pledge. Item five of the pledge read." As a Hindu I believe in the justice and necessity of removing the evil of untouchability and shall on all possible occasions seek personal contact with and endeavor to render service to the submerged classes."

The next most important event in the Vykom Satyagraha which was started in 1924 in Kerala to throw open the temple streets to the untouchables. But the people as well as the government were strongly against the movement. The Government of Travancore state put up barricades and prohibited the untouchables from entering the streets near the temple. In 1925, Gandhi visited Travancore state and informed the Government that, this act of theirs "was lending itself to the view that they were supporting the conservation of the Hindus of Travancore with their own physical forces." In April 1925, Gandhi wrote in young India, "For the opening of the roads is not the final but the first step in the ladder of reform. Temples, public wells and public schools must be open to the untouchables equally with caste Hindus." In response to this appeal, the Travancore Government removed the barricades but the opposition of caste Hindus went on unabated. How ever, Ayyappan writes, "The Vykom Satyagraha, though it had falled to produce any effect on the Travancore Government or the upper caste in kerala, made untouchability a problem of national importance". Another notable event was the conviction of an untouchable Murugesha, in 1926 when he entered a temple to offer his prayers. He was, arrested and convicted on the charge of defiling the temple. Gandhi was greatly moved by this incident and he wrote in young India, " It is simply fanatical obstinacy to persist in persecuting men in the sacred name of religion. Its persecutors who are knowingly defiling their own religion by keeping out of public temples men who are at least as honourable as they claim to be themselves, and are willing to abide by all the ceremonial rules".

On 2nd March 1930, ten days before Gandhi's Dandi March, Ambedkar launched a big temple entry movement at Nasik before the Kalaram temple. A huge band of 15,000 volunteers, including 500 women, was brought there to offer Satyagraha. The police anticipating violence, closed the gates of the temple and guarded them. A public meeting was convened to solve the problem peacefully. But the orthodox section was strongly against the temple entry. The Nasik Satyagraha brought great resentment among the people against the depressed classes and it went on until 1935.

After the rejection of the Simon commission report, the first Round table conference was convened in London in November 1930. The congress leaders were in jail so no representatives of the congress attended the conference. Ambedkar Attended and spoke about the loath some condition of the untouchables in India and said, "150 years of British rule did not alter even a little the position of the untouchables. They were prevented from drawing water from the wells, from entering into temples, by the caste Hindu society. The Government itself prevented their recruitment in the police and the military services on the ground that they were untouchables". This strong denunciation by Ambedkar brought the position of the untouchables into focus. Ambedkar prepared a declaration of fundamental rights safeguarding culture, religion, and economic rights of the depressed classes and submitted it to the minorities' sub-committee. He demanded the abolition of untouchability and the establishment of equal citizenship. He also demanded separate electorates for the depressed classes. The Karachi session of the congress was held in March 1931. In this session the congress adopted the fundamental rights resolution. Section 4 declared, "All the citizens are equal before law irrespective of caste, creed or sex". Section 6 declared, "All citizens have equal rights and duties in regard to wells, tanks, roads, schools and places of public resort maintained out of the state or local funds or dedicated to private persons for the use of general public". Section 10 declared universal adult suffrage. Thus, in March 1931, the congress finally liquidated the social institution of untouchability as far as it was concerned. At about this time, the Government of Bombay announced that members from the depressed classes would be recruited for the police department. This was an important result of Ambedkar's efforts.

On 14 August 1931, Ambedkar met Gandhi. They discussed at length the problem of untouchability. When Ambedkar Asked Gandhi about his opinion on the political rights of the depressed classes Gandhi said, "The political separation of the untouchables and the Hindus would be suicidal to the nation. Thus, there was no "bridge between the two leaders on this point.

Ambedkar and Gandhi left India to attend the second Round table conference in London. At the Minorities committee Gandhi declared, "we do not want the untouchables to be classified as a separate class". Members of the Round table conference were unable to agree to any solution of the minorities and communal representation including the political status of untouchables. British Prime Minister Ramsay Macdonald made it clear that the British Government would be forced to give its own award. On 14 August 1932, the British Prime Minister announced communal Award according to which the depressed classes were granted separate seats in the Provincial assemblies and they were given the right of double vote in which they could elect their own representatives and also vote in the general constituencies. Immediately Gandhi announced his resolution of fast unto-death in Jail. The declaration of fast-unto-death opened the eyes of the whole country towards this problem of the untouchables".

Madan Mohan Malaviya and others decided to hold a conference in Bombay on 19 September 1932 to resolve the deadlock and save Gandhiji's life. Malaviya wired to Ambedkar to Participate in the conference. On the eve of the conference, Ambedkar issued a statement asserting, "There have been many Mahatmas in India whose sole object was to remove untouchability and to elevate and absorb the depressed classes but every one of them has failed in his mission. Mahatmas have come and Mahatmas have gone but the untouchables have remained as untouchables".

Ambedkar demanded 197 seats as against 71 given by the award. Finally, the number of reserved seats was settled at 148, in the famous Poona pact. Immediately, it was transmitted to London and the British Government announced its acceptance. The Hindu Mahasabha also ratified it at its meeting in Delhi. Gandhi broke his fast on 26 September 1932.

Gandhi started his Harijan in 1933. In his message Ambedkar wrote," the outcaste is a by-product of the caste system. Nothing can emancipate the outcaste except the destruction of the caste system". However, Gandhi wrote that though many educated Hindus held such a view he was not able to share it. It was at this time that the Harijan sevak sangh was formed and the conference at Bombay pledged that the right to use the public roads, wells, etc., would be given statutory recognition when the swaraj, parliament met, in case such a legislation was not passed earlier.

Raj Gopalchari said, "in order to redeem the pledge of the removal of untouchability it was necessary to pass new laws. On November, 1932, the Madras legislative council passed a resolution unanimously that the Government should recognize the public sentiment and bring forward legislation to enable trustees to throw open temples to all Hindus. On 1 December 1932, Subbarayan, a former Chief Minister of Madras state, moved a Bill outlining procedure to enable the trustees to ascertain the will of the people regarding temple entry. With in a few days, Ranga Iyer moved a Bill in the Delhi Assembly on the lines of the November 1932 resolution of the Madras Council.

According to law, in all social matters the Governor General had to give his assent for moving the Bills either in the central or in the provincial legislatures. In January 1933, the Governor-General announced that he was not in favour of the two Madras Bills as they affected mary devotees who lives out side Madras state but who come to those temples. He, however, gave permission to Ranga Iyer to move the Bill in the central Assembly. Immediately, Ranga Iyer presented another Bill on the lines of subbarayan's Bill to ascertain public opinion. The Governor-General accorded his permission to move this Bill also.

Another very important incident took place in 1935 in Kavita, a small village in Gujarat. The Harijan workers in that village tried to get the Harijan Children amitted to the village school. But the Savarnas of the village were against it. Gandhi, in the Harijan of October 1935, wrote,

"The Kavita Savarnas had not recognized the time spirit". The Harijan workers offered to help the Harijans to leave Kavita so that they could settle down in another place, but they refused to leave their homes. Ambedkar was provoked by this incident and by the methods adopted by the Harijan workers to solve the problem. He attacked Gandhi that he wanted the Harijans to leave the village rather than launch cases against Savarnas. However, the Harijans succeeded a little letter in sending their children to the school because of the boldness of a Rajput living in the village. He visited the Harijan locality frequently and gave them moral support. As a result of this, the Savarnas changed their attitude and allowed the Harijan children to be admitted to the school. The instance also had a repercussion in the surrounding villages and the Harijan children were admitted to the schools in practically the whole area.

This incident brought out several features of the situation. Because of their upbringing and their prejudice, the Savarnas of the village were unable to tolerate the idea of their own children studying along with Harijan children in the school. For them Harijan children were more 'Harijan' rather than 'Children'. On the other side, the local Harijans were unable to revolt against the Savarnas again because of their upbringing and also because they constitute a minority in the village. Even when the Harijan workers offered to take them to another village where they could send their children to the school, the Harijan refused to leave their homeland. This is again a very typical reaction that they would rather put up with the humiliation than be uprooted. Finally, the incident shows how the determined efforts of a few savarnas brought about a change in favour of social justice.

Swift changes took place in the political situation in 1937 because the Congress party resolved to participate in the Elections. All the Congress candidates had pledged themselves to the removal of untouchability. In 1938, the removal of civil disabilities Act was passed by the Madras legislature which provided that no Harijan shall be disabled from any social or public amenity. In the same year, it also passed the Malabar Temple Entry Act which threw open the temples in Malabar.

In July 1939, at the instance of the workers of the Harijan Sevak Sangh and the Congress leaders, the temple at Madurai was opened to the Harijans. The opening of temples in other districts of Tamil Nadu followed this event. However, the orthodox sections filed civil and criminal suits. The Congress Government at Madras felt it necessary to condone the technical breach of law and it published an indemnity Bill for protecting the participants. Within a few months, in the same year, a temple entry Authorization and Indemnity Act, 1939, was passed by the Madras legislature authorizing the trustees to throw the temple open if in their opinion worshippers are not opposed to such an innovation.

Thus, Gandhi's fast and the Poona agreement had released tremendous forces throughout the country, which led to the removal of the disability of the Harijans. The 1937 elections clearly showed that the majority of the Harijan leaders throughout the country were with the Indian National Congress.

When elections were held in 1946 for the Constituent Assembly in the various provincial legislatures, Ambedkar found that the legislators in Bombay would not support him. They elected only the congress Harijans. He was able to get into the Constituent Assembly only with the help of the scheduled caste representatives. Later on, the Congress Harijan leader, Jagjivan Ram from Bihar, was nominated to the interim Ministry by the Congress, and Jogendranath Mandal, a member of the Scheduled Caste Federation, was nominated as the Muslim League representative in the interim Ministry. Thus, neither the Congress nor the

League was able to invite at this time Ambedkar who had hardly any followers among the elected Harijan leaders.

The Congress redeemed its pledge to the Harijans by declaring in the third session of the Constituent Assembly in April 1947 that, "untouchability in any form is abolished and imposition of any disability on that account shall be an offence." Not only the Indian press throughout the country hailed this declaration but also by the world Press. But the most dramatic event was that the Prime Minister, Nehru, invited Ambedkar to be the law Minister in the first cabinet of Independent India. Even moré significant was the appointment of Ambedkar as the Chairman of the Drafting Committee to draft the Indian Constitution.

Finally, the Indian Constitution, adopted ih 1950, proclaimed the principle of equality to all citizens irrespective of caste differences and made discrimination on the basis of caste justiciable in a court of law. Article 17 of the constitution abolished ineducability. As a result of this the Harijans enjoyed the same legal rights as any other citizen. Further adult franchise has given them political power. In 1955, the ineducability Act was passed fixing the penalties for infractions. Finally, the Hindu Marriage Act of 1956 removed the legal obstacles for inter-caste marriage. Thus, after long struggle by Gandhi and by Ambedkar and the organizations started by him on the other, the legal disabilities of Harijans were removed. Equality before law was assured.

6

Caste and Indian Constitution

The British Government fully exploited the caste system to keep the Indians divided and exploited caste loyalties to promote their own interests. In view of the harm done by the caste system, the leaders of India decided to check this evil in the post independence period. For this purpose they incorporated in the Constitution the ideals of justice, equality, liberty and fraternity. Several provisions of the constitution, particularly the preamble, part III, Fundamental rights and part IV, directive principles of State Policy, clearly reflects the constitutional strategy for securing social justice.

The constitution grants right to equality to all persons, which includes:-

(a) Equality before Law. All are equal under law. The state shall not deny to any persons' equality before law. (Art-14)

(b) The state shall not discriminate against any citizen on grounds only of religion, race, caste, sex, place of birth or any of them. (Art-15) Further Article 15{2] prohibits discrimination on the grounds of religion, race, caste, sex, or place of birth; nor can any person on any of these grounds be held able or disable for access to shops, hotels, public restaurants and places of public entertainment or the use of wells, tanks, bathing ghats, roads and places of public resort maintained wholly or partly by the state funds or dedicated to the use of general public.

(c) Equality of Opportunity for all citizens in matters of public appointment. No citizen shall on grounds only of religion, race, caste, sex, descent, place of birth, residence or any of them, be ineligible for, or discriminated against in respect of any employment or office under state. (Art-16)

(d) Abolition of untouchability- Article-17 abolishes untouchability and forbids its practice in any form and makes it a punishable offence in accordance with law for those who practice untouchability.

(e) Abolition of titles helps to develop social equality and uproot the inequality that existed in the society prior to independence between the people of upper and lower classes. (Art 18)

(f) Right to freedom to peruse any business trade or profession or career. [Article-19]

(g) Special protection for weaker sections of society- women, children and persons belonging to scheduled castes and scheduled tribes. Art 29 (2)

The other steps taken to curb the caste evil include introduction of universal adult franchise and termination of separate electorates. Article 326 of the Indian constitution provides for universal adult suffrage. In this system, the adults irrespective of discrimination on grounds of caste, class, sex, creed and religion shall have the right to vote and choose their representatives through periodic elections.

A significant step taken by the framers of the constitution is the abolition of communal electoral. Communal representation which had brought untold miseries and unfortunate partition of the country, has been banned. Of course, reservations of seats are made for the scheduled castes and the scheduled tribes and for the Anglo-Indians for a temporary period to uplift them. The legal provisions are embodied in Part XVI of the constitution of India entitled, Special Provision Relating to certain classes".

For these special categories of person, the constitution makers provided for different level and types of concessions. Under Article 330 and 332 seats, in Lok Sabha and Vidhan Sabhas were required to be reserved on the basis of their population. It was initially available for ten years, but subsequent amendments to the constitution, this period has been extended from time to time and are still in force. For the Anglo-Indian community, the facility of reservation of seats in Lok Sabha was also provided that, two seats will be nominated by the president of India, in case he found that this community did not have enough representation.

The other category of special provision under part – XVI relates to appointment to services and posts. For the scheduled castes and scheduled tribes under article 335 posts are to be reserved according to their population. Article 336 provides reservation for Anglo-Indians in union governments services of railway, custom, postal and telegraph for ten years as they were available to them immediately before Independence.

Article 46 of the constitution of India which deals with the Directive Principles of State Policy enjoys the state to "Promote with special care the educational and economic interests of the weaker sections of the people and in particular of the scheduled castes and scheduled tribes and protect them from social injustice and all forms of exploitation".

Article 164 provides for a ministry of tribal welfare in Bihar, Madhya Pradesh and Orissa where, as noted above, nearly half of the tribal people live. The provision of the sixth schedule of the constitution gives considerable degree of social, cultural and political autonomy for the tribal areas of Assam. These areas were divided into districts according to the groups. These districts were autonomous. It is also provided that when there are different tribes in a district, the Governor is empowered to divide the area into autonomous regions. Each district and each such region will have its own council of not more than twenty-four members, of whom not more than three-fourths shall be elected on adult suffrage.

Similarly, part Ten of the constitution of India deals with "the scheduled and tribal areas" and the details of administration are given in the fifth & Sixth schedules.

According to the fifth schedule, each state which has scheduled tribes living in, it must establish a tribal Advisory council. Consisting of not more than twenty members of whom about three-fourth shall be the representatives of the scheduled tribes in the legislative Assembly of the state and othér members of those tribes.

Recognizing that the Indian society is made up of hundreds of millions of citizens who are utterly poor, illiterate and living in small, closed tribal and village societies, the constitution had laid stress on social, economic and political justice along with equality of status and of opportunity in the "Preamble".

Article 340 empowers that the state to investigate the condition of the backward classes and to help them by grants etc. Thus, the constitution has accepted the following elements of backwardness, illiteracy and lack of education, poverty, exploitation of labour, non-representation in services and untouchability.

As regards the socially and educationally backward classes, now popularly called 'OBC' the only provision for them is under Article 340 of the part – XVI of the constitution. On the recommendation of the mandal commission 27% of posts are reserved for OBC in central and state services.

The constitution has made provisions to safeguard the interests of the scheduled castes and scheduled tribes. Article 338 lays down that there shall be a National Commission for Scheduled Castes and Scheduled Tribes to be appointed by the president. The function of this commission is to investigate all matters relating to the safeguards provided for the scheduled castes and scheduled tribes under the constitution of India. The president shall cause all such reports to be laid before the parliament. The commission reports on the administration of the scheduled areas and the welfare of the scheduled tribes in the states. The commission reports any matter of atrocities (against the scheduled castes and schedulers tribes) to the union Government and the union shall give direction to the state Government to take up measures for the welfare of these people.

The provision for the appointment of minister-in charge for looking after the welfare of schedule castes, scheduled tribes and other backward classes in the state of Bihar, Madhya Pradesh and Orissa, also reflects indirect recognition of caste factor.

Though the spirit of secularism stands clearly affirmed in the constitution, yet in a limited and indirect way it recognizes the caste system in the form of providing for the reservation of seats for SC, ST, OBC and Ango-Indian community.

The reservation systems on caste basis have come under strong criticism. Sociologists like I.P. Desai, Upendra Baxi, and Andre Beteille opined that reservation should on the basis of economic class instead of caste. Caste based reservation is against the basic spirit of our constitution which promises equality, non-casteist and non-communal secularism and a non-obscurantist society. The criticisms of reservation system notwithstanding, there are equally cogent arguments in its favour. Marc Glanter, D.L. Seth and many others have not only justified the system but have also favoured the continuance of caste-based preferences for years to come. Reservation provide a direct flow of valuable resources to beneficiaries in larger measure than they would otherwise enjoy. Reserved seats, for example, provide an important legislative presence and swell the flow of patronage, attention and favorable policy to scheduled castes and scheduled Tribes. Thus the caste-based policy of reservation, with all its criticism, has enough to command in its favour.

Basic Contradiction in the Constitutional Provision

The sole aim of the constitutional provision is to uplift the backward classes so that they may enter the main stream of national life as early as possible. Article 14 guarantees to all citizens and others equality before law. All citizens enjoy equal protection of law. "The state shall not deny to any person equality before law or equal protection of the laws within its territory." But the structure of Indian society including Hindus, Muslims, and Christians, is based on caste hierarchy and inequality. This is the basic contradiction in the current Indian situation even after half a century after the adoption of the constitution.

The Indian social structure is based on caste and all the social, educational and economic disabilities arise as a result of the practice of caste inequality. Each caste is structured on the basis of endogamy and so preserves its identity. The people belonging to caste want to preserve caste identity, but fight against caste hierarchy. Further each caste wants to rise up and claim equality with the castes above but is against the castes below coming up. So each caste whether 'backward' or 'more backward' or 'depressed' desires that the reservation of seats in colleges and jobs in the government should be on the caste basis. But the advanced castes while preserving the caste identity desires that the principle of equality should operate so that with the advantages of education and influence they are enjoying, they can maintain their forward status and give only lip sympathy for the upliftment of the masses. The concept of 'social justice' sounds hollow when we take into account the realities of social life.

7

The Backward Classes and Social Change

Two thirds or more of the populations of India are very backward, being illiterate and living in utter poverty. There are three broad divisions among the backward classes: (a) The Scheduled Castes (Harijans) (b) Scheduled Tribes (Garijans) and (c) The other Backward Class. The SC and ST are listed in the constitution while the other backward class is unlisted and loosely defined; it is the least homogeneous. As a result, the problem of other backward classes is very complicated and very difficult to deal with. While it is possible to have an all India list of SC on the basis of untouchability and the scheduled tribes on the basis of their way of life, it is impossible to have any such list for the Other Backward Classes.

The Position of Scheduled Castes

One of the earliest references to this group appears in the *Chhandogya Upanishad* which uses the term "Chandala." The term referred to a degraded person who is ranked along with the dog and the pig. Buddhist Jatakas of the second century B.C. also speak of the Chandalas as a despised group living outside the village, who speak a special dialect and have their own hereditary occupation. The Dharmasastras declare the Chandala to be the progeny of a Brahmin women and a Sudra man. Manu also declared that these people lived outside the village and that they were prohibited from entering the villages and towns in the day time. These statements are confirmed by the observations of Alberuni, who wrote in about 1020 A.D. He noted the Dom and the Chandala as the two groups who did the dirty work like cleaning the village and who were distinguished by their occupations.

But it is very difficult to imagine that persons born out of forbidden sex contacts were numerous enough to form a separate caste group, since they are to be found practically in all the villages of India. It is possible that because they were following occupations, which were despised, they were characterized by the Dharmasastras as equivalent to the despicable progeny of forbidden sex relations. As G.S. Ghurye in his book "caste, class and occupation", writes, "Ideas of purity, whether occupational or ceremonial, which are found to have been a factor in the genesis of caste are the very soul of the idea and practice of untouchability". Thus, because they were following occupations like scavenging, doing leather work, removing dead cattle from the village, and so on, they were looked upon as a profane group, contact with whom was defiling. So they were required to live in a separate colony outside the village.

The practice of untouchability was at its worst in different parts of the Kerala state in the South-West corner of the country. As A. Aiyappan writes, "while the belief in human beings as carriers of graded degrees of ritual impurity is common to all Hindus, these manifestations are nowhere as hypertrophied as in Kerala. To avoid upper castes being polluted, the distance at which the polluting castes have to remain has been fixed and prescribed by tradition". Among the untouchables also there are various castes; the distance at which these castes had to remain, varied from about 30 feet to about 150 feet. According to Ambedkar, these groups persisted in practising Buddhism even after the bulk of the Hindus gave it up and so they were banished from the villages. This view also appears to be rather far-fetched.

In the opinion of B. Kupuswamy, "It looks as if these groups of people were declared untouchable and were made to live outside the village for two reasons. First, they were following the lowest kinds of occupations like Scavenging, leatherwork, removal of the carrion, etc.; and second, they persisted in eating beef, which was condemned as the most heinous crime by the caste Hindus. As Srinivas notes, "They are an integral part of the village life, they perform certain essential tasks in agriculture, they are often village servants, messengers and sweepers, and they beat the drum at village festivals and remove the leaves on which people have dined at community dinners".

The Position of Scheduled Tribes

Seven per cent of the total populations are leading the tribal way of life. According to the scheduled tribe lists, modification order 1956 there are 414 different tribes in the various states in India. In respect of scheduled tribes Chhatishgarh, Jharkhand, Orissa have the largest population.

One of the chief difficulties is the problem of definition. The Government of India have taken the simple step of listing the tribes and have called them the scheduled Tribes. A tribe is an indigenous homogenous unit speaking a common language, claiming a common descent, living in a particular geographic area, backward in technology, preliterate, loyally observing social and political customs based on kinship".

The economic status of the tribes very all the way from poor food gathers to agriculturists, plantation labour, and industrial labour. The kadars; the Malapantaram, the Paniyans of Kerala, the Paliyan of Tamil Nadu, the Kudukurubas of Mysore are dependent on forest products. They are essentially food gathers. They collect fruits, edible roots and honey from the forest and supplement these with hunting or chase of animals. Where there are ponds and rivers they catch fish.

The bulk of the tribal population of India depends on some form of agriculture with forest produce as secondary support. The oraon, the Munda, the Bhill, the Santhal, the Majhwar, the Kharwar, the Baiga, the Korwa, the Gond and the Ho practice shifting axe cultivation consisting of feeling the trees on a hillside a little before the monsoon and setting them on fire. When the earth is covered over by a layer of ashes and when the rains fall, they scatter seeds and with an occasional shower of rain the seeds take root and grow. But the crops are scarce and are of an inferior quality. The soil becomes impoverished in the absence of ploughing and manuring. So they sift to another valley and cut the trees there. This process of agriculture besides being inadequate, is very wasteful as it leads to deforestation and soil erosion and floods. So the forest laws prevent shifting cultivation. This leads to terrible hardship to the tribal people. Further, land alienation is the most important problem affecting these groups.

Many of the tribes are good at handicrafts which include basket mating, spinning and weaving. There are some functional classes among the saore, the Kond, and the Gond who devote themselves to metal working, cane working, pottery, weaving and so on. The Tribal people of northeastern states have an economy midway between the food gathering and primitive agriculture. Their social and economic organizations are built around their cattle, which form the economic, as well as the religions basis of the life of the tribe.

Other Backward Classes

The Backward Class movement started in the early part of the twentieth century, when schools and colleges were giving courses in secular subjects through the medium of English, only the castes and classes with the tradition of education utilized the opportunity to educate themselves. As a result only the members of these castes and classes could get the jobs in the Government services and increase their prestige. This further increased the cultural, social and economic distance between them and the lower castes. This made the lower castes to realize that they were nowhere in this situation. They wanted a share in the new opportunities. As Srinivas himself puts it, the lower castes realized that mere Sanskritization was not enough. It did not provide them the avenue for social mobility and obtain well-paid and prestigious jobs in the administrative services. So they desired to get themselves educated through the English medium in order to qualify themselves for the new jobs in the administration and new profession like law, medicine, engineering etc. Srinivas further says, "It is no accident that the movement was strongest in peninsular India, where only one caste, the Brahamins enjoyed and preponderance in higher education, the professions and Government employment. It is also the area where a wide social and cultural gulf obtained between the Brahmins and others."

However, it was soon realized that the qualified youth could not get admission in the professional courses and the post-graduate courses because admission was based on marks in the High School and college examinations. Here they were at a handicap since the boys from the homes with education as a tradition were able to secure high marks. Another complication arose as a result of the fact that the teachers and examiners were from the forward castes. This gave rise to the fear that they were being discriminated against on the basis of caste. A similar situation arose when they competed for jobs in the Government services. Here also the appointing authorities at the lower levels were mostly Brahmins. With not very high marks and with the prevalence of nepotism, the young men from the lower castes found themselves at a disadvantage. This led to anti-Brahmin feelings both among the leaders of various lower castes and the frustrated youth. Thus the aim of the backward class movement at this stage was to limit the Brahmin monopoly in the two fields of education and appointment to Government posts. As Srinivas writes, "The opposition to Brahmin dominance did not come from the low and the oppressed castes but from the leaders of the powerful, rural dominant castes such as the Kammas and Raddis of the Telugu country, the Vellalas of the Tamilnadu and the Nayar of Kerala." These were high caste groups with a social position next to the Brahmins. They included not only the Hindus but also the Muslims, Christians and other Communities. This is the important reason why the term used to describe these groups is "Backward classes" and not "Backward castes".

Experience in the last quarter of a century has clearly shown that the number of groups in the list increases rather than decreases with the time. Concessions create a vested interest in backwardness. No group wants to forego the concession; it is because no group as a whole can truly say that all its members have now become 'forward' that no section of the group needs special concessions. It is true that, when the leaders of these groups put forward the case in the parliament, their arguments are neither untrue nor unjust.

The Backward Class Commission was appointed in 1953 with Kaka Kalekar as the chairman. The commission was appointed according to the Article 340 of the Constitution. The commission was asked to determine the criteria to be adopted to provide concessions to "Socially and educationally backward classes" besides the Scheduled castes and Scheduled tribes. The commission was also asked to prepare a list of such classes. Inaugurating the commission, the late prime minister Nehru said that he disliked the term "backward classes" since ninety per cent of the people were poor and backward.

One of the first recommendations of the commission was that the 1961 census should provide caste wise figures so that "before the disease of caste is destroyed all facts about it have to be noted and classified in a scientific manner as in a clinical record". The committee also recommended that certain sections of the Muslims, Christians, Sikhs should be included among the other "Backward Classes".

As regards causes for backwardness, the commission has concluded "A" variety of causes-social, environmental, economic and political-have operated both openly and in a subtle form for centuries to create the present colossal problem of backwardness. Economic backwardness is the result and not the cause of many social evils".

With respect to criteria of backwardness the commission recommended for general guidance:

1. Low social position in the traditional caste hierarchy.
2. Lack of education in the major section of the caste or community.
3. Inadequate or no representation in government service.
4. Inadequate representation in the field or trade, commerce and industry.

SOCIAL CHANGE AMONG THEM

One significant features in the twentieth century has been the weakening of the barriers between the sub-caste and the barriers arising out of pollution. Higher education, Government employment, and urbanization have led to the crumbling of the sub-caste barriers. The endogamous circle widened and educated people tended to look upon the barriers of the sub-caste as not insurmountable when it came to finding suitable brides and bridegrooms for their children. This was also due to the new movement of

All-India Caste Conferences, which fought for the consolidation of caste in the country as a whole and the breaking down, of the sub-caste barriers. It may be mentioned that the caste system, as it was practiced, restricted the choice of marriage not only to the caste and the sub-caste but also to the sub-caste with in the linguistic zone and even there practically with in the district or the neighbouring districts. The All-India caste conferences worked against these regional, linguistic and sub-caste barriers. A third-movement responsible for the weakening of the barriers was the nationalist movement which launched mass campaign under the leadership of Mahatma Gandhi. His Campaign against untouchability lead to the weakening of the notions of pollution.

Some of the tribal people like Santhals, the Kond and the Gond from Bihar, Chhatisgarh, Jharkhand, Orissa and Madhya Pradesh have migrated in large numbers to Assam to work on the plantations. The areas in Jharkhand, Chhatisgarh, Orissa, Madhya Pradesh, and West Bengal, which are rich in coal, iron, etc., have led to the emergence of industrial labour. It is estimated that about half of the labourers in the manganese industry of Madhya Pradesh are tribal people. The Santhal and the Ho are prominent in the Bihar iron industry. Nearly the entire unskilled labour force of the Tata Iron and Steel Co. are tribals. There is both the inside "push" following economic hardship due to land alienation, indebtedness and outside pull due to demand for labour in tea plantations and in industries. Thus, the tribesmen have been transplanted from the tribal life to the urban life and so are confronted by great difficulties in social adjustment.

As D.N. Majumdar puts it "Today most of these tribes have come in contact with advanced communities, have learnt traits of their neighbours, have borrowed patterns of their dress and developed an intricate material economy. Some of these tribes have progressed at a tremendous pace effecting in a few years changes which have taken centuries to achieve in other areas".

These contacts have arisen, in a number of ways. First, the itinerant vendors from the neighboring villages and towns who have taken clothes and trinkets, metal utensils, patent medicines to the hills and the Jungles; Second there are administrative officers who have gone into these areas because of the forest laws and revenue laws. Third, there were Christian Missionaries who wanted to convert them to Christianity in order to save their souls. Fourthly, all types of contact have been greatly increased because of the tremendous developments in transport and communication. Finally, the existence of mineral resources in and around primitive tracts have led to the establishment of mines, industries, and educational institutions.

As a result of these cultural contacts, there have been changes, in their food habits, dress, ways of living etc. and the various tribes of India are now living at different cultural levels. Some of these tribal groups however, continue to line even now in seclusion, comparatively uninfluenced by these cultural contacts. But some of the groups have adopted the Hindu customs because of their association with the village people. Others have been converted to Christianity. But the large majority of the tribal groups in India have now more or less settled down in the rural areas taking to agricultural and other allied occupation.

However there was a school of thought which favored isolation. Another school particularly advocated by the social reformers and voluntary organizations, was one for assimilation of these tribal groups either into Christianity and Hinduism. The Christian missionaries and some social reformers like Thakkar Bapa have recommended this. The third view, which is actively followed in the recent years; is that of integration. The policy of integration aims at developing a creative adjustment between tribes and non-tribes of India leading to responsible partnership.

In conclusion, it may be pointed out that a big social change has come among the Harijans (SC) and to Girijans (ST) on the basis of the temple entry legislation, the reservation of seats in Parliament and the state legislatures, the provision of educational facilities and employment opportunities. During the last fifty years, thousand of SC & ST families have moved from the lowest class to the middle class. Thousands of them have been members of the legislature in the state and central parliament, some persons chief ministers & president of India etc. Further, as it has been noticed earlier, the Government has taken caste as the basis for the upliftment programme.

On the other hand, the practice of untouchability is in its virulent form in the villages where 80 per cent of the population live. Caste is the most important dimension in the social structure of the village and the members of the Harijan castes are too few in the village to fight for their rights and too divided among themselves to consolidate their limited strength to fight for their rights. Thus the one big change in the position of the Harijans (SC) is that in the urban areas on the basis of their education, employment and income, they are in a position to move into the middle class, but in the villages it is impossible for them to experience any change in status.

8

Dominant Caste

In many parts of India the rural life is marked by the existence of dominant castes. For a caste to be dominant, it should own a sizeable amount of fertile land locally available, have strength of members and occupy a high place in the local hierarchy. When a caste has all the attributes of dominance, it may be said to enjoy decisive dominance. There may be occasionally more than one dominant caste in a village. Over a period of time one dominant caste may be replaced by another. The power and prestige of the dominant caste affect its relations with other castes, including the ritually superior. Srinivas in his writing says that, "caste may be said to be dominant when it preponderates numerically over the other castes and when it also wields preponderant economic and political power. A large and powerful caste group can be more easily dominant if its position in the local caste hierarchy is not too low. When a caste enjoy all the elements of dominance it may be said to be dominant in a decisive way. The followings are the important factors of the dominant caste.

(i) High Ritual status.

(ii) Numerical majority

(iii) High economic position, and

(iv) Relatively high education or occupation position.

The elders of the dominant caste in a village were the watchdogs of a pluralistic culture and value system.

Traditionally, they prevented the members of a caste from taking over the hereditary occupation of another caste. The only exceptions were agriculture and trade in some commodities. The dominant castes, then, maintained the structural distance between the different castes living with in their jurisdiction. Many of the rules they upheld and enforced were local rules. The role of the dominant caste was not, however, restricted to being the guardian of a pluralistic culture. It also stimulated in lower castes a desire to intimate the dominant caste's own prestigious style of life. Dominant castes did set the model for the majority of people living in rural areas, occasionally including even the Brahmins.

T.K. Oommen in his article says that, the problem I have discussed so far may be grouped into three categories. First of all some methodological questions were raised. The element to be included in the definition of dominant caste, the need to locate, the crucial variables in defining dominant caste and the distinction between the possession of resources for the exercise of power and its actual exercise. I also suggested that the inclusion of political power as an element of dominance should not be allowed to result in confusion between means and ends.

Secondly, he has discussed caste in theoretical assumption. He has given some notable features of a dominant caste. They are:

(i) That dominant caste is a united group.

(ii) That power is concentrated in one or another caste.

(iii) That power is mainly as an ascriptive attribute.

The third set of points he has made to relate the inadequacy of the notion of dominant caste in grouping with the changing social realities of rural India. Democratic decentralization, organisational innovations, market economy, spread of literacy, introduction of adult franchise are all effecting rapid transformation in Indian rural society. The notion of dominant caste was developed on the basis of empirical data collected in the late forties and early fifties. Whatever right have been its validity in the past its usefulness as an analytical tool seems now to have been greatly diminished.

T.K. Oomen has thoroughly discussed the role of caste in politics. He says that some times caste becomes important for politics. Most of the studies by the political scientists and the political sociologists are usually developed with out accounting for the role played by the forces of social structure. Sociologists and social anthropologists observed that caste is an institution of prodigious potentially. Religion and region are fruitful forces, all of which eatup into the very vitals of secular politics. They go to the extent of suggesting that the instrument of adult franchise had facilitated the particularistic forces to consolidate themselves and to reinforce them. He says about three broad forms of political recruitment.

(i) Recruitment on predominantly particularistic grounds in which traditional factors weigh heavily.
(ii) Predominantly charismatic recruitment in which personality factors figures prominently.
(iii) Predominantly charismatic recruitment in which ideology orientation and commitment is the leading consideration.

He further says that voters cast their votes on the basis of caste, religion, linguist or local affiliations of the candidates and not on the basis of their understanding of policies or how they would benefit the country's economic and social development.

Carolyn Eliott says that Reddies and Kammas in Andhra Pradesh are economically rich, politically strong and numerically more. The most important source of their power is to control over land. They are major landholders. With these resources, Reddis and Kammas has become the political leaders of the village. The competition for power takes place between groups formed for the purpose other then politics in which political leaders reach prominence initially through resources of power other then political authority. But political leadership of dominant caste is not solely a reflection of other forces. Political power in the villages depends not only in material ties of dominance and obligation but also on qualities which add to economic power differentiating the wealthy political leader from the wealthy individual in the village.

Hardgrave in his study of Nadars in Tamilnadu says, " Nadars of Tamilnadu considered by high caste Hindus in the early 19th Century to be among the most defiling and degraded of all castes. The Nadars suffered several social disabilities and were one of the most economically depressed communities in south India, in their response to the social and economic changes. However Nadars have become one of the most economically and politically successful communities in south. In the field of trade and education they are unexcelled and in politics the power of Kamraj Nadar extends across the whole of India.

Some of the castes included among the other backward Classes are very powerful in the economic, social and political fields though large proportions of their members are not as well educated as the advanced castes; nor are they well represented in the Government Jobs. Being powerful lend-owners and the traditional village headmen they are very powerful in the political field at the local, district and state levels. Among them are the vokkaligas and lingayats of Karnataka state, Nayars and Ezhavas of Kerala state, Vellalas and Nadars of Tamil Nadu state some of them are high caste groups, immediately below the Brahmins in status and with a relatively high English education. The members of these castes have been able to utilize the funds provided by the central and state Governments for the award of backward class scholarships, the funds allotted for agriculture development and have also been successful in securing jobs of prestige in the Government offices and are powerful in the legislatures and in the formation of the state cabinets.

There have been cases when the dominant caste have shown vigilance against any infiltration of low caste. There have been several cases of ill treatment and torture. The torture some times results in the killings of low caste. William Rowe has reported a case. According to his account the Noniyas (salt makers) of Uttar Pradesh who are engaged in digging well and making bricks and tiles all on a sudden decided to put on the sacred thread enmass. This was offending to the kshatriyas who gave order to beat the Noniyas and tear off the sacred thread by force. A collective fine was imposed on the Noniyas. A few years later the Noniyas again repeated the same thing, but were not given any punishment. In the second time the Noniyas did not put on the sacred thread amass at a time, they donned it one by one secretly. There after the Kshatriyas tried to prevent the process through the Government, but in vain.

There was another example of Ahirs who tried to get themselves enumerated as Kshatriyas in the census report of 1921 and donned the sacred thread. By doing this they annoyed the dominant caste. In North Bihar the Bhumihar Brahamins tried to prevent the attempt of the Ahirs. It resulted in violent clashes and the matter went to the court. Another example was reported from the Ramnad district in Tamilnadu where the Harijans made similar attempt.

One of the big problems facing the present society is the fact that these dominant castes have developed a vested interest, which enables them to enjoy all the benefits. They resist all attempts to take them out of the other backward class lists, since they are now fairly well advanced and since the funds and opportunities available should be utilized for the benefits of the castes which are more backward. This is one of the reasons why the various commissions try to develop criteria to distinguish between the backward castes' and the more backward classes., But, these caste groups do not want to give up the advantages; it is a fact that though some members are quite forward, the majority of them are yet poor and illiterate; they would like these sections of their castes to get the benefits. Also they are eager to retain these advantages for their own benefit.

As a result new tensions are being generated between these "Powerful backward castes" and the "Weak backward castes" as well as the schedule castes. There are now signs of these two latter groups joining their forces to fight, what may be called, the advance backward castes. Thus, it may be said that, a new backward class movement is now emerging. Probably one of the important reasons for the rise this new awareness among those belonging to these sections is the realization that in the rural areas the dominant castes are keeping them in subjection. A new polarization is emerging between the advanced section of the Indians, which include the lower castes, the Muslims, the Christians and other minorities. This polarization was in evidence in Karnataka State towards the end of 1973 when the advanced sections joined together and condemned one of the Harijan Ministers who was out spoken against exploitation of backward groups by the forward groups; the other sections joined together in supporting him. Another evidence of this was the conveying of the backward class conference in Bangalore in which representatives from all these sections from the four Southern States participated.

9

Casteism in Indian Politics

India is a democratic country. The Government here runs by representatives of the people elected by periodic elections. This process of open and direct election has provided much grounds for caste to have it firm imprints on the Indian soil. Castesim has often dominated the political parties, this influencing the electoral process. The attitude and behavior of the political leaders have some times become caste-oriented. Caste affects the political behavior and values of the leaders which influence electoral process in the following ways.

First, political parties often choose candidates for the constituencies on the basics of the castes which have much influence in the constituency.

Secondly, generally people of one caste is motivated by vote for a candidate of same caste.

Thirdly, further in selecting the candidates, Caste is taken as one of the factors for consideration.

Fourthly, when a single caste group does not get much support, it forms alliances with other groups against the major groups in society.

Indian society is caste based society. In the selection of candidates in a political party it plays a vital role. Hastmann in the analysis of Indian political parties is of the opinion that party is nothing but it is the organizing intermediary forces in which parties are such a mechanism which integrate the plurality of society and this action model is a political, which creates consensus for maintaining democratic way of life. By this means the function of political parties is to break and control the consequences of disintegration tendencies. He strongly held that in India without parties the integration process can not be realized because of parties stand as the social of intermediary between State and society. In other wards it can be said that political parties are significant in linking State with individuals. Apparently, a number of functions performed by the smaller political parties cannot be political oriented but they are determined by the structural elements of society. This process does not includes social heterogeneity because of languages, religion and ethnic groups or castes. These heterogeneity forms typical structure within the functional political system.

Caste provides a basis for the emergence of several interest groups in the Indian system each of which competes with every other group in the struggle for power. At times it leads to unhealthy struggle for power and acts as a divisive force. However it is a source of unity among the members of various groups and acts as a cohesive force. In rural India, where the social universe of the rural power is limited to an area of 5 to 10 K.m., caste acts as a unifying force. It is the only social group they understand. However, the existence of two or three big caste groups also leads to factionalism. Caste as such is a factor in Indian politics and it acts as a cohesive as well as divisive factor.

M.N. Srinivas says that "The features of caste prevailing through the past centuries may be described under the nine following heads – hierarchy, endogamy and hupergamy, occupational associations, restriction on food, drink and smoking distinction in custom, dress and speech, ritual and other privileges and disabilities of caste organisation and caste mobility. He says that in the villages political and social entity brought together members from different castes. Srinivas also says that, mostly land holders are belonging to higher castes groups. This type of caste group are dominant politically as well as economically and this has led to the exploration of the connection between economic and political power through the analysis of local political system and discussion of the extent to which class and party interest link.

V.M. Sirsikar also says that castes play a key role in Indian politics. In his opinion caste is the traditional integrative agency of the political party. Caste is playing new role of regulating political behaviour. A Brahmin does not perform only the traditional priesthood functions. He adopts the westernized way of living, but he remains to the core so far as his personal and political life is concerned. This secularization of power of caste does not represent its decline. In India it is possible to change religion but not the caste. In the conflict between castes and political parties is the fight between social institution having a standing of thousand years and political parties with barely a life of few decades. More over Indian political parties are weak in both organizational structure and ideological fabric. Majority of political parties exploit casteism for their own purposes is undoubtedly true No prophecy is possible regarding the date when caste would disappear from the social political life of this country.

Chetkar Jha also considers caste as an important factor for Indian politics. He says that, unlike religious communalism, casteism has been operating though organized political parties. Only a few political parties are explicitly organized to represent castes. In practice all parties apply caste arithmetic in distributing and balancing tickets among a variety of castes. Each caste group leaders with in a party wants that the maximum number of party tickets should go to the members of his own caste, so that his position would be strong. Parties also keep in view of the caste composition of the constituencies and castes of the contesting candidates personal and other qualities of the candidate would be considered when more than one candidate comes for the same caste.

Pauline Kolenda has also discussed the significant role of caste in Indian politics. He says that India has been an effective democracy since independence. Following the examples of western democracies political parties wage electoral campaigns and winning election has become a principal means of gaining power in modern India. At first it appears that caste block voting would emerge as an important phenomenon. Dominant castes transplanting their local variables and influence into the arena of state electoral politics. Caste associations are also playing key role in many affairs of life. Some caste associations have participated effectively in politics.

The formation of caste associations is an important innovation introduced by the dominant groups of the castes to maintain their hegemony and to protect their interest. To broaden their support base, some of the caste associations have been stretched into caste federations. In order to bind together the caste members, the caste associations occasionally pass resolutions ventilating grievances of the caste against the Government. Some of them launch welfare programmes which includes loans, Scholarships etc. for the deserving members of the caste. These organizations no doubt seek their basis in caste identities but they are primarily interested in political power for securing their economic benefits.

According to Rudolph and Rudolph, "by providing bases for leadership and representation the horizontal organizations of castes with common identities have contributed significantly to the success of political Democracy". They have enabled the members of middle and low castes to find basis of self-esteem. As pressures from caste groups and caste associations have increased tremendously.

Rajani Kothari says that, Indian system can be described as a system of one party dominance. In India the congress which is the party of concensus functioning through an elaborate network of factions which provides the chief competitive mechanism of Indian system. In 1947 the congress which functioned as a broad based nationalist movement before independence transformed itself into the dominant political party of the nation. Opposition in India is for all practical purposes a regional phenomenon.

He further says that politics is an instrument wielded by a particular stratum in a society to consolidate or raise its position, its function in to reproduce or modify existing status of superior subordinate relationship. But in particular case of caste and politics even this is partly relevant where caste itself becomes a political category. It is futile to argue as to whether caste uses politics or politics uses caste. He gives three dimension of caste system:

(i) Secular Dimension:

In many regions it was Brahminic section that first responded to English education and were the first caste to benefit from political and administrative power.

(ii) Integrative Dimension:

Political age however emphasizes both, the traditional emphasis on studies of caste system of differentiating and affirmed segmentation has neglected the integrational dimension.

(iii) Dimension of consciousness:

It is more effective in modernized sector.

He further says that, in some other regions where Brahmins were never so dominant, certain agricultural upper caste wielded power. But in this respect he is not fully agree that only caste is everything. He says that where castes are large, are not homogenous, and where they are small are not enough for numerical force. Secondly, one caste alienates to other castes. Thirdly, political parties gain stability only by involving all major sections of the community. An impression prevails that where as things like education, urbanization and industrialization were making in roads into traditional sectarian loyalities, etectoral polities have resassociated them and reestablished their legitimacy and that this has given rise to disintegrative tendencies that will disrupt the democratic and secular frame work of the Indian politics.

F.G. Bailey has analysed political activity at three levels: The state, constituency and villages. There are only three among possible levels. He says that if these three can be satisfactorily handled this will provide a method of handling other areas as well. Anthropologists having been long in contact with societies, which are orderly and yet have no Government, have ceased to limit their definition of political to such institutions as kings and parliaments and political parties.

Rushikesh Maru says that numerical strength is important factor for organizing a party and for winning the election. He says that when one numerical strong caste is oriented to one party other numerically strong caste will look to other party. He says that in Gujarat the antagonism to the congress had made the kshatriyas more conscious than over before of the need to build an organized mass base through politics.

Caste did not enter politics all at once with independence, but it made its presence strongly felt in the first general election, and increasingly with each successive elections. Even after the subject 'caste and politics' had been taken up by scholars in various disciplines in the 1960s and

1970s, some differences remained between the ordinary run of social scientists who saw and stressed the importance of caste in politics, and what are called 'late intellectuals' who were inclined to treat it lightly.

As Srinivas showed caste came to be used in the electoral process from the first general election, and indeed it had entered the political arena even before. But the question is not simply of the extent of the use of caste in electoral politics, but also of its meaning and legitimacy for the different sections of Indian society. Clearly, those who yielded to the appeal of caste loyalty and voted for candidates of their own caste, could not have all thought that it was a bad thing to vote according to caste. By and large, the intelligentsia showed an, ambivalent attitude. They were troubled by 'casteism' in politics even though they might support some one from their own caste.

In the 1950s and 1960s, the leaders of all political parties condemned in public the use of caste in politics. Politicians freely acknowledgea that caste was being extensively used in the politics of post independence India, but they said that it was being used by other parties, not their own. When it was shown that their party too was using caste, their reply was that they did not start the process but were being forced to accommodate caste in order to survive, for in polities, or at least in Indian politics, one could not afford to be too idealistic if one wished to remain in business. In other words, they sought to defend the use of caste on tactical rather than ethical grounds.

A change in the orientation of political leaders, and with them of other members of the intelligentsia appears to have started in the 1970s when the politics of backwardness took a new turn with the installation of the first non-congress Government in New Delhi in 1977. It began to be argued that caste needed to be given a place in public life not so much on grounds of Real politic as on grounds of social justice. The lower castes had been stigmatized and exploited in the past, and they should be given special protection through extensive quotas in every domain of public life. The argument was not new; it had been an important component of colonial policy in the decades preceding independence. What was new was its increasing appeal to social justice and its increasing vehemence.

Again, we can not enter into a discussion of the principal features of the politics of backwardness of which others have written extensively, but would like to point out that it has acquired a markedly ideological tone since 1990. The ideological tone was given a new articulation when the left parties decided to join hands with V.P. Singh's Janata Dal in pressing for the extension of caste Quotas in the cause of social justice. It was impossible for any party to oppose caste quotas openly. Neither the supporters nor the opponents of caste quotas said that caste itself should be revitalized. The issue for that moment was not how caste has altered polities, but how politics altered caste. Edmund Leach had already asked more than thirty years ago whether castes cease to be castes when they compete with each other for political power. There were obvious and significant continuities between the castes of the present and those of the past, something to complex and deeply-entrenched as caste does not cease to be itself as soon as one or even a few of its basic characteristics change.

Three Stages in the Relation Between Caste and Politics

Rajani Kothari, a political scientist has specified three typical stages in the relation between caste and politics in a region.

Stage –1

This involves the politicization of a powerful elite caste, usually one which responded earlier to the opportunities for western education. In Maharashtra and Tamil Nadu, this was the Brahmins', in Bihar it was the Kayasthas. With some political success on the part of the entrenched caste, the members of other high castes in the area would respond with resentment, feelings of relative deprivation and possibly antagonism. These castes then challenge the entrenched caste as what Kothari call an "Ascendant Caste." The three examples given in Kothari's edited book, the "Ascendant Caste" is one of the respectable cultivators who had been slower then the 'entrenched' caste in accepting western education. In Rajasthan, the Rajputs were the 'entrenched' and the Jat cultivators were the 'ascendant' caste. In Tamil Nadu, the Brahmins were the entrenched, and the Shudra non-Brahmins were ascendant and in Maharashra, the Brahmins were the entrenched and the Marathas were the ascendant caste.

Stage 2

Factionalism and fragmentation take place with in the competing castes, and multi-caste and multi-factional alignments develop. Lower castes are often brought into support high caste leaders and to strengthen a faction.

Stage 3

Caste identity tends to languish with the progress in education, urbanization, and the development of an orientation towards individual achievement and modern status symbols. Individuals participate in network which includes persons of several castes. In the words of kothari, " The structure of particularistic loyalities has been overlaid by a more sophisticated system of social and political participation with crosscutting allegiances. Institutional differentiation and specialization has progressed, so that economic, political, educational institutions are distinctly different."

The Indian sociologist, G.S. Ghurye, raised the spectre

of a future with Indian society fixed in stage-2- composed of a few blocks or coalitions of castes. This could occur through the gradual break down of rules of exogamy between castes of neighboring rank, so that each connubium was enlarged to include several castes of adjoining rank. If this happened, the French social anthropologist, Louis Dumont, sees a result, that would be disastrous, for one would end up by aggregating multitude of small groups into a few large blocks, which would be mutually hostile and exclusive to a dangerous degree.

Dumont believes that such blocks of castes would not be ranked or interdependent, but would be, rather a universe of impenetrable block, self-sufficient, essentially identical and in competition with one another.

Whether Ghurye's or Kotharis vision is correct is hard to say. Kothari suggests that identifications other than that of caste are likely to become more important with advancing education, urbanization and adoption of a modern achievement orientation. The D.M.K. party in Tamil Nadu is the only important political Phenomenon resembling such a block of castes as Dumont speaks of the party is composed of many members of the high Sudra castes and is explicitly anti-Brahmin. The Republican party is composed very largely of untouchable Mahars of Maharashtra, but it includes other untouchables in central and northern India. It has not yet wielded much political power. If all castes were distributed among a few major blocks contending for power through election and Governmental institutions, there would be a new caste system based on a principle of competition.

Louis Dumont is one of the out-standing French students of caste system in India. His book " Homo hierarchicus " has been recently translated from French to English. He shows that the caste system is based on the fundamental social principles of hierarchy. Both the principles of equality and of hierarchy are facts of modern, social and political life. In his opinion the two great ideals of modern life are the freedom of the individual and the equality of men. The three basic features of caste system, namely-heredity, hierarchy and endogamy negate both these ideals.

Hierarchy by itself is inescapable in any human society. The unique feature of the caste system is that hierarchy is based on birth. An individual is knit with emotional ties with the group in which he is born. Secondly hierarchy is based on the principle of purity and pollution; the pure is superior to the impure; the pure and the impure must be kept separate; thus arises the operation of the principle of endogamy. The system is further complicated by territorial factor, even when the caste and sub caste are the same, the different territorial groups do not intermarry. According to Dumont, caste endogamy is an expression of the principle of separation: Marriage, commensality and contact with members outside the group are forbidden, with varying degree of strictness in that order. All these rules are governed by the caste panchayat which has the power to excommunicate the family which violates the rules.

ANTI-BRAHMIN MOVEMENT IN POLITICS

For over one hundred years, there were specifically anti-Brahmin political movements, the earliest in Maharashtra in the mid-nineteenth century. In recent decades, such movements have been strongest in the South Indian states of Tamil Nadu, Karnataka and Kerala, where laws relating to Government run universities have been written to pointedly discriminate against Brahmins. These laws are a reaction to the dominance of Brahmins in Government service and to the disproportionate number of Brahmins among students in institutions of higher education upto 1920. In south Indian Brahmins has also been large land owners and thus had secular as well as religious power.

Early in the twentieth century, there developed in

south India a strong Dravidian movement. The Dravidian chauvinists argue that there was a casteless Tamil culture in south India before the Christian era. According to the movement's interpretation of history, the Dravidians then allowed themselves to be dominated by the Brahmins and their teaching. During the 1950s the Dravidian chauvinists adopted an ant-Aryan attitude towards North India. In the 1960s, the DMK in Tamil Nadu raised the demand for secession from Indian union and the creation of an independent Dravidnad. The DMK demanded a separate Dravidian state which would be casteless and egalitarian. The D.M.K broke away from the Dravida Kazagham in 1949. Early anti-Brahmin parties included the justice party founded in 1916, the self-respect movement founded in 1925 and the Dravida Kazagham (DK) founded in 1944.

The demand of DMK for an independent Dravidnad, however, failed to involve the majority of the Tamils and even led to the division in the DMK when persons opposed to secession formed the Tamil National Party (TNP) under E.V.K. Sampath. The congress was also in a position to maintain its support base in Tamil Nadu and it apposed the demand for Dravidnad. The Government of India took a tough stand. The constitution of India was amended in 1963 to deal firmly with persons indulging in secessionist activities. Oath of allegiance to the constitution of India was made compulsory for all the candidates seeking election to union and state legislatures. Thereupon, the DMK leadership decided to abandon the demand infavour of the creation of a Tamil union but its members did appeal to regionalism and were eminently successful in 1967 in winning seats at all levels of government in Tamil Nadu. The DMK was not so successful in 1972, but still it is the only major political party explicitly anti-caste and composed of members almost entirely from one division of castes-the high sudra castes. Whether the D.M.K will become a caste model party for future is difficult to say. As early as in

October 18, 1975 Mrs Indira Gandhi, thus, summed up the situation: "Caste has become not so much the old system of gradation of people or professions, but it has almost become an instrument of political and economic confrontation, whether it is in elections or it is some thing else. People do try to exploit this, fortunately not always very successfully."

Frankly, never before has these been so much emphasis on caste-Jat and non-Jat, Reddy and Kamma, Rajput and Bhumihar, Harijan and non-Harijan as there is to day. And never before has the Indian leadership reduced politics to caste game as it has done now. The top leaders, who proclaim the goal of a casteless society, now openly organize caste oriented rallies in the states to display their clout and ability to be in the Public focus.

Some of the political parties like DMK and Republican party of Maharashtra have recognizable caste bases. In a few cases, conflicting caste groups find shelter under the same political umbrella. Then there are non-Political caste based organizations. During the 1990s, Ram Vilas Paswan set up an all India action committee on behalf of the scheduled castes, scheduled tribes, the backward classes and the minorities to assert their constitutional rights' to reservations.

Since 1967 politics at the regional level has become more and more caste oriented. Though appeals in the name of caste are barred in law, party leaders and party candidates use it as a tool to win support for elections. Ever since its victory in the local elections of 1967, the caste based DMK and ADMK has usually held the chiefministership in Tamil Nadu. In Punjab, where the main dynamic has been between the two leading, parties the congress and the Akali Dal, their leadership has usually been in the hands of the Jat Stalwarts: Pratap Singh Karion, Gurunam Singh, Prakash Singh Badal, Surjit Singh

Barnala, Beant Singh etc. Even in west Bengal where it is claimed that "caste plays no role in politics", the reality is altogether different. Of the total 43 members of left front state cabinet in 1984, as many as 17 bore high caste Brahmins Surnames, 12 high caste kayasta surnames, one high caste vaidya surname, and the two upper middle caste surname. Even today the political power is primarily under the command of upper caste. What to talk of non-leftist political parties in India, our left leaders, whether of CPI, CPM or the CPML are mainly drawn from high castes possessing the very trait they condemn in others.

According to Andre Bateille, "politicians in some states have no doubt learned to manipulate caste in the furtherance of their interests. But politics is a dynamic Phenomenon. Hence politicians, whose only skill is caste politics are likely to become absolute".

The Caste Association and Politics

The caste association, a voluntary organization composed of members from a single caste, was also viewSed by political scientists as a potentially important political instrument. The caste association could demand candidates or concessions in return for support by the caste. Also, through the association the urban politically-literate elite were link with the less literate villagers belonging to the same caste.

Caste associations linking members of a caste with in a region first emerged in the nineteenth century. Such associations became possible as education became more accessible and easier means of communication and transportation were established. Often, the associations were funded by western-educated male members. These organizations published newspapers and held conferences to discuss discrimination suffered, reform of customs and the establishment of benefits such as scholarships and hostels for their student members.

Some caste associations have participated effectively in politics. Lloyd and Susane Rudolph described the way in which the Vaniya Kula Kshyatriya Sangham (the vasiya caste Kshatriya association) a caste association in Northern Tamil Nadu, was able to support political parties and strike political bargains resulting in their representation in the state legislature in a relatively high number. In order to bind together their caste members, the caste associations occasionally pass resolutions demanding their grievances before the Government.

A caste association must solve a number of problems if it is to be successful in politics.

First, the population is fragmented into so many castes that even a dominant caste in a region does not constitute a majority of the electorate.

Second, few castes are organized-adequately to mobilize all members of the caste to vote as a block. An associations ability to deliver the vote can be undermined rather easily by the opposition parties putting up candidates form the same caste.

Andre Beteille notes that in Tanjore district of Tamil Nadu, where the largest caste is the Kallas, all parties put up Kalla candidates. Such techniques tend to defeat the power of the caste association as a political organization. Since it is narrowly identified with one caste, the organization can not attract the support of voters of others castes unless it abolishes its exclusiveness and thus ceases to be a caste association.

The above account clearly illustrates the dominant role of caste in politics of India. Caste loyalties and other ethnic factors and not ideological differences really divided Indian Political Parties. The Indian Party system and the electorate clearly reflect the caste division. Without going into details regarding the good and bed effects of caste on politics in India, it can be said that the introduction of representative democracy based on the principles of one man, one vote has brought caste into the ambit of Politics. The various caste groups generally claim their right to participate in the elections and contest for power. According to Rajani Kothari. "It is not politics that gets caste-ridden. It is caste that get politicized. People belonging to schedule caste and schedule tribes use politics to keep intact their constitutional protections and privileges or reservation seats and jobs and educational opportunities". Morris Jones rightly remarks, " the central discovery is that politics is more important to caste and castes are more important to politics than before".

Caste is a hindrance to national integration. It encourages divisive and factional forces and thereby affects national unity. The educated and the illiterates, the rich and the poor, infact the people living in all parts of India still remain attached to their castes despite liberalization of restriction on diets, marriage and residence. The caste factor continues to be a determinant of Indian politics. It continues to act as one of the chief means by which the Indian mass has been attached to the process of democratic politics. The politics of reservations has also tended to give strength to the forces of caste in Indian politics.

Although the subject of caste and politics was initially of interest to only a handful of social anthropologists, it soon attracted the attention of political scientists and others, and there is now a large literature on it. Today, many more scholars, both Marxists and non-Marxists acknowledge the importance of caste in politics, although they drew different policy conclusion from it.

10

Caste as Determinant of Political Participation

The political behaviour of an individual is a part of the totality of his behaviour. A political being is not isolated. He lives in society and all the social forces phenomena shape the condition of his behaviour. Both the political and social world supply inducements to him to act in a particular way. Thus, the political aspect of his life can not be separated from social, economical, religious and educational aspects of his life. He is a member of a family, follower of a particular religion, member of a caste and its sub-caste, member of a economic group and as well as a constituent element of a particular pattern or structure of political process.

Although there are studies on caste and politics, but studies dealing with caste as the determinant of political participation are meager. Hence the present writer has focused upon this aspect of the important area of inquiry.

Political participation is the involvement of people at various levels of political process. Although the political participation relates to both the input and out put functions of a political system the present writer's study is confined to the input aspect of the political system.

The scopes of study in terms of respondents are confined to five hundred families. Four villages were selected for the study. These villages are in the Aska Lok Sabha constituency of Ganjam District in Orissa. The scope in terms of area covered in the research are limited to rural areas of the district of Ganjam. The scope interms of subject matter included the analysis of Bio-social profile of respondents, caste as the determinant of political participation and nexus between caste & politics.

Ganjam District

The history of Kalinga vis-à-vis Ganjam virtually starts from the time of Mauryan Emperor Asoka who made a devastating invasion to Kalinga in 261 BC and defeated Kalingan. After this war, Kalinga was included in the Mauryan empire, Tosali and somapa (identified with Jaugada in Ganjam district) was made the capital and subsidiary capital and ancient routes were linked with kalinga and Magadha and also other provincial capitals. The present Orissa comprises the old Kingdoms of Utkal, (Cuttuck & Puri district) Odra, (Dhenkanal and Angul district) Kangoda, (Khurdha district and Banpur) Kosala (Sambalpur and Bolangir districts) and Kalinga (Ganjam district and the north-east portion of Andra Pradesh). Of all the coastal kingdoms like Odra, Utkal, Kongoda and Kalinga, the latter played a vital and conspicuous role in all phases of its history, culturally and politically. Ganjam district was all along included in kalinga region witnessing the theatre of civilization and embracing the cultural waves of the south, north and west. The state Deity or Rastra Devata Jagannath is stated to have originally belonged to the savara tribe of Ganjam.

Perhaps during the reign of Ibrahim Qutab Sahi during 1571, the Persian term Ganj-1-Aam (Ganjam), meaning the granary of the world, was coined. The undivided Ganjam district was amalgamated into Orissa in 1936 after its separation from Madras Presidency. The Ganjam district comprises three subdivisions namely Brahmapur, Chhatrapur and Bhanjanagar-Subdivisions. It is one of the littoral districts of Orissa on East coast. The major river of the district is Rushikulya.

Chhatrapur is the district headquarter. The district is divided into two parliamentary constituencies i.e. Aska and Brahmapur. Prominent leaders like Biju Patnaik, P.V. Narasimha Rao and Nabeen Patnaik were elected from these constituencies. In reality, Aska had become the political bastion for Biju Patnaik at the fag end of his political life. Four villages selected for study were BARAGAON, KENDUPADAR, BALISIRA and CHERAMARIA of Aska parliamentary constituency.

Village no I selected for the study was Baragaon. The total population of the village was 4491. Among them 1038 people were scheduled castes. The scheduled castes mostly comprise of Keuta (fisherman), Kumbhar (potter), Bauri and Hadi (untouchable Harijans). The OBC population were 1123 which comprises mostly Aliya Khandayats, (swordsman from Ali kingdom of erstwhile Utkal or present Cuttack district of modern Orissa) 50 Bhandaris (barbers), and 5 sonars. The rest 355 were Shasan (priestly) Brahmins and Balabhadra (cultivator) Brahmins.

Social Structure of Baragaon

Sl. No of caste		*No of caste families*	*Percentage*
1.	Shasana Brahmin	3	0.69%
2.	Balabhadra Brahmin	25	5.81%
3.	Alia	270	62.79%
4.	Barber	10	2.32%
5.	Teli	01	0.23%
6.	Keuta	50	11.62%
7.	Sunari	01	0.23%
8.	Bauri	70	16.27%
	Total	430	

The second village selected for study was Nalabanta of Nalabanta Grampanchayat of Aska Block. The population of the village were 2757. Among them 565 were scheduled castes, 690 were Brahmins and rest 1502 were OBC castes. The Brahmin group comprises of Sashan (priesty) Brahmins and Sarua (cultivator) Brahmins. The OBC group consists of Banayat Odiya (cultivating caste), Kalanji (Bravery swordsmen who were soldiers of Kalinga and fought the Kalinga war in 261 BC), Bhandari, (barber), Gouda (generally having cattle and selling milk), Ranguni (Bunakar), Muni (sebayat) and Maharana (carpenter). The scheduled caste group comprises Bauri, Hadi (untouchables Harijans), Keuta (fisherman) and Dhoba (washer man).

Social Structure of Nalabanta

Sl. No of caste		*No of caste families*	*Percentage*
1.	Sarua Brahmin	270	36.88
2.	Sasana Brahmin	30	4.09
3.	Banayat Odia	200	27
4.	Kalanji	10	1.3
5.	Bhandari (Barber)	10	1.3
6.	Gouda (Cattleman)	30	4.9.
7.	Ranguni	20	2.73
8.	Muni	2	0.27
9.	Maharana (carpenter)	10	1.3
10.	Keuta (Fisherman)	30	4.9
11.	Dhoba (washerman)	10	1.3
12.	Bauri & Hadi (untouchables)	110	15.2
	Total	732	

The third village selected for study was Balisira village of the same Grampanchayat of Aska Block. The total populations of the village were 2164. Among them 295 people were scheduled castes, which comprises Hadi, Bauri, Dhoba and Keuta. 541 were high caste people that include Shasan Brahmins and Karans (Pattnayaks). The rest 1328 people were from OBC castes, which comprises Dalua (cultivators), Kalanji, Bhandari, and Kumuti (Kalinga Vaisya Traders).

Social Structure of Balisira

Sl. No of caste		*No of caste families*	*Percentage*
1.	Brahmin	180	26.54
2.	Dalua	320	47.19
3.	Kalanji	60	8.84
4.	Bhandari	20	2.94
5.	Karana	04	.58
6.	Kumuti	24	3.53
7.	Hadi	70	10.32
	Total	678	

The fourth village selected for study was Chermaria of Nalabanta Gramapanchayat of Aska Block. The total populations of the village were 542. Only 40 people were scheduled castes and the rest were Gouda and Kalanji Khandayats. There were no Brahmins in the village.

Social Structure of Cheramaria

Sl. No of caste		*No of caste families*	*Percentage*
1.	Kalanji	50	48.54
2.	Gouda (cattleman)	40	38.83
3.	Bauri	10	9.7
4.	Bhandari (Barber)	2	1.94
5.	Dhoba (washerman)	1	0.9
	Total	103	

Interview schedule was the main tool used in the present study for the purpose of information. The method of sample survey was employed for the purpose of investigation.

TABLE 1

Participation of Respondents in Voting at Different Levels of Political Process in Relation to Their Caste

Voting	*Response*	*Brahmins and High castes*	*OBC and middle castes*	*S.C/S.T.*	*Total*
Parliament	Yes	110	87	30	227
	No	90	38	45	133
Assembly	Yes	114	84	110	308
	No.	91	41	60	192
Panchayat	Yes	175	112	135	422
	No.	30	27	21	78

TABLE 2

Respondents Who Took Collective Decision Regarding Voting in Their Family

Collective decision	*Brahmins and High castes*	*OBC and middle castes*	*S.C/S.T.*	*Total*
Yes	70	61	100	231
No.	43	41	42	126
Total	113	102	142	357

TABLE 3

Respondents Who Exercised Their Right to Vote Freely

Response	*Brahmins and High castes*	*OBC and middle castes*	*S.C/S.T.*	*Total*
Yes	45	21	15	81
No.	78	65	133	276
Total	123	86	148	357

TABLE 4

Caste Preferences of Respondents

Response	*Brahmins and High castes*	*OBC and middle castes*	*S.C/S.T.*	*Total*
Candidates of own caste	88	40	73	201
Candidates of other caste	12	17	17	46
Able candidates	21	15	17	53
Party candidate	14	11	12	37
Village Heads advice	12	14	15	41
Supported by largest No. of villagers	14	13	19	46
It depends upon the situation	16	13	11	409
Total	177	123	164	464

TABLE 5

Respondents Involved as Party Worker

Activities	*Brahmin and high caste*	*OBC and middle*	*SC/ST*	*Total*
Put on party cap/badge	12	8	9	29
Distributed leaflets	12	7	9	28
Conversed from door to door	5	4	6	15
Participated meetings procession	1	1	2	04
Carried voters to polling booth	5	3	6	14
Extended financial help to candidate	1	—	—	01
Acted as polling agent	1	1	—	02
Total	37	24	32	93

Table 6

Political Discussion in Family

Political Discu-ssion in family	*BR. High*	*OBC & M.*	*SC/ST*	*Total*
Yes	150	96	82	328
No	39	38	95	172
Total	189	134	177	500

TABLE 7

Political Discussion with Family

Political Discussion	*Brahmin and high caste*	*OBC and middle*	*SC/ST*	*Total*
Yes	180	94	120	394
No	11	08	87	106
Total	191	102	207	500

TABLE 8

Objective of Political Discussion with Family

Objective of political discussion	*Brahmin and High caste*	*OBC and Middle*	*SC/ST*	*Total*
To influence others	136	59	26	221
To get influence	36	26	50	112
To inform others	76	65	18	159
Total	248	150	94	492

TABLE 9

Respondents Regarding Regular Meetings of Gram Sabhas

Response High	*Brahmin and Middle*	*OBC and*	*SC/ST*	*Total*
Yes	30	25	22	77
No	109	42	100	251
Total	139	67	122	328

TABLE 10

Respondents for Not Contesting Panchayat Elections

Reason	*Brahmin and high caste*	*OBC and middle caste*	*SC/ST*	*Total*
Not for common man	35	25	30	90
Dirty politics	19	15	10	44
Lack of education	20	21	38	79
No majority of our caste	29	26	30	85
No time	32	21	84	137
It is for high caste people	—	12	29	41
Other cause	5	4	5	14
Not responded	3	3	4	10
Total	143	127	230	500

TABLE 11

Reasons for Not Becoming Party Member

Reasons	*Brahmin and High caste*	*OBC and Middle Caste*	*SC/ST*	*Total*
Not pursed	90	40	43	173
Reluctance	98	30	39	167
No party member	2	—	1	3
Poverty	10	20	58	88
Politics is a dirty thing	22	16	17	55
Government service	5	4	3	12
Old age	10	6	8	24
Such need never arose	12	7	12	31
No time	38	37	60	135
Not responded	9	12	23	44
Total	296	172	264	732

Democracy is a system of government in which people can take part directly or indirectly in the decision-making process. It gives an opportunity to every ordinary man to do extraordinary things. It involves a 'consensual-participatory culture' and 'the consensual-participatory allocation of values'. It is the theory of mass-action, mass-access and mass-involvement. But direct democracy is not possible in the modern territorial states. The only alternate to adopt is indirect representative democracy where people elect their decision makers after a certain period of time.

A democratic system does not act itself. The successful functioning of democracy largely depends on the active participation of people. Political participation implies a hierarchical ranking of behaviour. The social-hierarchy, in which every individual has a defined place by birth, is based on caste gradations. It is a system of 'institutionalized inequality' which results in 'cumulative inequality.' It is a closed system of Hindu social life. Thus, caste is of great importance as regards the political participation. Firstly it is anti-democratic feature and secondly, due to the policy of 'protectional discrimination', the low caste people are now acquiring much greater influence and power through the political participation.

Like caste, religion is also an important determinant of our way of living and thinking. Hindus are in overwhelming majority and Islam's are minority community in India. Moreover caste system prevails only in Hindu society. Therefore the influence of caste on political participation will be analyzed on the basis of Hindu caste system.

Caste and Voting Behaviour

In India, there is universal adult suffrage. But the people legally equal are not equal socially. It is therefore, quite possible that the low-caste people may find it difficult to participate in political life because of their social conditions and because of their lower socioeconomic position, they may not get an easy access to the more important forms of political participation as compared to the high caste Brahmins. The participation of people at the different levels of political process is an index of democracy. A society may be highly egalitarian or hierarchical in relation to the political participation of the people. If the anti-democratic social system of community largely influence the working of democratic institutions, the democratic claim of the community can not be sustained.

The right to vote is the right to significant share in political power. It assumed that the high-caste people have ruled over the low-caste people for ages and if they wish to keep themselves in power they should be more keen about taking part in voting, as in a democratic system, it is this act of voting which decides who are to rule over the people for a definite period of time. As regards religion, the Muslims and Christians are in minority compared to the Hindus. As democracy is a system of majority rule, the minorities try to share power or try to keep themselves associated with the decision- makers by involving themselves more in political acts so that their interest may be protected against any possible tyranny of the majority. It is obvious that the minorities are more keen about exercising their right to vote than their majority counterpart. This case is also applicable for the high caste and low caste people in India. In other words, the low caste people are keener about exercising their right to vote than their high caste counterparts.

It is evident that democracy has brought a fundamental change in the ways of living and thinking of the low – caste people. Thus, it is a sense of newly acquired dignity and equality that actuates them to participate in voting more than their high-caste counter parts. The underlying reason for lower participation of the high caste may be their belief that democracy has undermined their superior traditional position and has brought them at par with those over whom their ancestors had been exercising power for ages and to some extent they themselves have also exercised that control over them.

Caste and Local Politics

Generally the influence of caste and religion is predominant in local election i.e. in Panchayataraj election. However it is alleged that the high caste people still try to maintain their traditional superior position in the villages. It is, therefore, assumed that the high-caste people are more likely to take part in the local elections than their middle and low caste counterparts. But the enhanced social status has enabled the lower castes to function in the political area as well. In some elections, in some states, and in some communities, caste has a peculiar significance as determinant of politics. For example, in States like Haryana, UP and Bihar, where majority of the voters are Jats, Rajputs, Thakurs and Yadavs, the caste factor determines the results of the local elections.

Family and Voting

In the case of certain castes in our country, the role of the family is predominant and if any member of the family violates the norms of caste-behavior, all family members are socially and economically punished by the caste groups. Generally this is evidently true in the case of the low caste people. Thus, the low caste people are more in favour of taking collective decision regarding voting with the consent of all family members than their middle and high caste counterparts.

It has already been established that in rural India, it is the family which is more important in matters of voting than a voter's individual inclination. Mostly all the family members vote for the same party or candidate. But in certain castes the control of the family on its members is higher than it is in others. It is generally, high in the case of the low-castes. Generally it is true that the high caste people are more likely to exercise their right to vote independently than their middle and low-caste counterparts who are under much control of family.

Political Preferences

Political Preferences are often intimately connected with caste and communal considerations. It is alleged that political parties in India are neither secular in their politics nor in organizational patterns. The parties, which may be termed as secular, do not hesitate in exploiting the communal sentiments of people. If the BJP has been supported by the high caste Hindus, the Congress, Bahujan Samaj party, Rastriya Janata Dal has been getting the backing, generally of the Harijans and Muslims. The political preferences of the individuals may, therefore, be said to be closely connected with the caste and community.

The Congress party, after the independence emerged as the party of the masses and all sections of society extended their support to it, but recently it has changed its attitude and seems to be more committed to the well being of the down–trodden and Muslims and to a socialistic programme. Therefore the hypothesis is that the Harijans and Muslims are more likely to wish for the victory of the Congress party than their high caste counterparts.

Caste and Communal Consideration

Every individual by birth belongs to a particular religion and caste which determines, to some extent, his political behavior. In order to ascertain the extent to which the people are governed by the caste and religious considerations in matters of voting, the question given below has been put before us.

Supposed there are two equally qualified candidates contesting election from your constituency and one of them belong to your caste and the other does not. Would you like to vote for the candidate belonging to caste or not?

Certainly, the answer will be in favour of voting for a

candidate of the caste. Less will prefer to vote for the able candidate. Thus, it may be concluded that the people in the rural areas have a soft corner for the candidate belonging to their caste in matters of voting.

Caste and Election Campaign

Party members are supposed to do the campaign work of their party during the time of elections. Besides the party members, each party entrusts the campaign work also to influential persons, who are not party members, for strengthening the position of its candidate. As the high caste people in the rural India are considered more influential, it is therefore, assumed that they are more likely to have acted as the party-workers than their middle and low-caste counterparts. The low and middle-caste people are more likely to involve themselves only in the simpler election activities as they are socially backward and are not in a position to make greater sacrifice in terms of time and money.

Caste and Political Discussion

It is assumed that the high caste people are better informed due to their superior social position and greater-accessibility to the means of mass communication. They are, therefore, more likely to discuss political matters than their middle and low-caste counterparts. Generally people like to discuss political problems more with their family members as Friends Company is more conducive to political discussion than family environment. This is generally true in the case of the rural people.

The high caste people in our society have for ages enjoyed a privileged position in all walks of life and that feeling of superiority is still found in them. They, therefore are more likely to inform others or influence others whether they assume the role among friends of equal status or among those who are inferior to them to social, economic or educational matters. Thus, it may be concluded that the high caste people have been involved in political discussion with friends in order to influence others. But the low caste people have been involved in political discussion in order to get information.

Caste and Party Membership

It is, generally, alleged that political parties in India are controlled by the high caste people. But it is true that the high caste people are more likely to be members of political parties than their middle and low-caste counterparts. But the time has been changed. The percentage of low-caste as party members, now a days, is greater than that of the high caste people. The underlying may be that the low caste people enjoy all types of facilities provided by the government under the constitution, which are not available to the middle caste people. It is, therefore, quite possible that their enthusiasm is comparatively, greater than that of the middle-caste people who are unprivileged or under-privileged in our country. The high-caste people are more socialized and politicized because of their own efforts and the low caste people are being socialized and politicized by the efforts of the government. The supremacy of the high-caste people seems to be declining under the present democratic system which is based on equality and the policy of protective discrimination, the position of the middle and low caste people are inevitable in the party organization.

Caste and Assembly/Parliament Election

Seeking election for the panchayat, legislative Assembly and parliament bodies requires that one must be economically sound, capable of sparing time for public service and commanding the support of the people. Besides, he should fulfill the constitutional requirements necessary for the office. It is assumed that high-caste people, due to their superior, social, economic and educational position, and low caste people (SC/ST), due to constitutional safeguards and reservations, are more likely to contest elections for the village council, the state Assembly and parliament. Besides it should kept in mind that contesting election for a body higher in the hierarchical organization of the democratic structure of the country, involves greater costs in terms of time and money than that of the bodies which are lower in hierarchy. The significant point to be noted that the traditional factors are more powerful at the local level as compared to the constitutional safeguards. But in state and national politics the traditional factors are not so effective as the constitutional safeguards. Thus, it may be concluded that in case of village politics, the traditional hierarchical supremacy still persists.

All caste people wishes to contest the village council election will show two reasons the first for the service of the people and the second important reasons is the betterment of village life. Thus, the sense of service and village uplift are the principal driving motives for contesting the village council elections. On the contrary, the important reason for not contesting elections by the low caste people are lack of majority strength of the caste and lack of time. Besides, illiteracy, politics a dirty thing and politics is a business of high caste people are other reasons. The belief that contesting the elections is not for the common man is dominating among the high caste people. The lack of minority strength of the caste and illiteracy are the dominating reasons in the case of the middle and low caste people. Thus, it may be said that the caste is an important determining factor in electoral victory in elections and it is not possible to win elections with out a caste majority.

Caste and Meetings of Village Council

There is a common complaint against the working of the village Assemblies and councils that regular meetings of these bodies are not convened. Similar complaint is that the high caste people are more likely to take part in the meetings than their middle and low caste counterparts. It is assumed that the high caste people are more actively involved in the local politics where they can exert their traditional supremacy on the middle and low caste people.

If the meetings of the village Assembly are not held regularly, the fault does not lie with the institution but with the men who run it. The voters of the village Assembly are constitutionally empowered to ask the Pradhan [village head] to convene a meeting. The low caste people are never interested to ask the village president to convene a meeting. It may, therefore, be said that attending the Gaon Sabha meetings has been a function of high caste people.

Democracy rests upon the belief that all power belongs to the people, who exercise it by a many sided-participation in public affairs based on the principle of equality. However, legally equal men and women may not be equal other wise. Uneven distribution of resources makes it possible for some to take the lead over others.

The study of caste and political participation is of utmost importance in a democratic state like India as it implies an active cooperation of all the caste, creed, religion and linguist in the management of the government. Its study has got a special significance in a society where democratic principles, norms and symbols are being motivated by caste factors.

Political participation as 'the involvement of the people at various levels of the political process' is hierarchical in nature and depending upon the nature of act, requires participation of all castes from top to button.

Man is not an isolated being. The social setup in which he lives exercises a decisive influence on his political behaviour. But this does not mean that the political setup has nothing to do with political participation. The nature and significance of political participation vary from caste to caste. Thus, it may be concluded that the caste is a decisive factor in the village politics. It may be said that political behavior, like other human behavior, takes place in the context of the social milieu, political setup, economic condition, historical background and cultural heritage of the caste. But, factors like political beliefs, ideologies and emotional issues are not to be ignored while building up a theory of political behavior.

The study of caste as the determinant of political participation shows that the release of an individual form the traditional bonds of family, kinship, caste, religion and neighbor hood is neither complete nor universal. The democratic values are, no doubt, shattering the anti democratic beliefs and norms of Indian society. However, the quantitative aspect of political involvement indicates that on the whole, the people have been extending their support to make democracy a success in India.

If all caste people are not actively involved in the political process, they alone should not be blamed for it. It shows that the operational instruments of democracy (mainly political parties) are not effectively and efficiently performing their functions. They are weak in their organizational and functional aspects. It is a function of political parties to persuade the people to share the responsibilities of the government.

The belief that politics is a dirty thing and voting a device to be fool the people, can easily be removed from the minds of the low caste people by their representative and the whole time political workers. This can be achieved by dedicating themselves to the selfless service of the people and by keeping themselves away from narrow and parochial motives.

11

Caste and Reservation Politics

The aim of the backward class movement was to limit the Brahmin monopoly in the two fields of education and appointment in Government posts. However, this was by no means a mass movement. Srinivas says, "The opposition to Brahmin dominance did not come from the low and the oppressed castes but from the leaders of the powerful, rural dominant castes such as the Kammas and Reddis of Andhra Pradesh, the Vellalas of the Tamilnadu and the Nayar of Kerala." These were high caste groups with a social position next to the Brahmins. They include not only the Hindus but also the Muslims, Christians and other communities. Incidentally it may be noted that most of the Muslims and Christians are converts to these religions from the lowest castes; their conversion to these religions does not enable them to overcome their social disabilities particularly in the villages and in the city slums.. The term backward class is very old. It has been in usage since 1917 when the Indian National Congress resolution emphasized 'the necessity of justice and rightness of removing all disabilities imposed by custom upon the depressed classes".

The great controversy of the fifties, regarding the steps to uplift the backward classes, so that they can enter the mainstream of social and economical life of the society, has centered around the determination of (a) the unit and (b) the criteria. As regards the unit, the nationalist elite and the localist Brahmin elite are in favour of the logical democratic unit of the individual as the basis, while the localist non-Brahmin and minority community elite are in favour of the caste as the basis. With respect to the criterion again the nationalist elite and localist Brahmin elite are in favour of income being the criterion because it is a universal criterion, while the localist non-Brahmin elite are in favour of caste as the sole criterion.

The Nationalist elite are afraid that if caste is taken as a basis to determine who should get the concessions regarding opportunities for higher education and Government jobs, the society will be fragmented. The localist Brahmin elite are against caste being a criterion since their opportunities for education and appointment will be narrowed by the concessions given to the powerful and numerous lower castes.

The localists non-Brahmin elite are afraid that if the universalistic economic criterion is used, their opportunity will be limited by the large number of well qualified but poor Brahmins who will enter the competition and walk away with the concessions. Thus, the real conflict is between the localist Brahmin elite and localists non-Brahmin elite. By and large, the Nationalist Brahmin elite are universalistic and egalitarian in their outlook. But the localist Brahmin elite are particularistic and caste oriented in their daily lives but universalistic in their outlook. This is the threat of universalism perceived by the localist non-Brahmin elite, they feel that in the name of universalism and egalitarianism the localist Brahmin elite want to perpetuate inequalities and exploit the situation to consolidate their own position and leave the vast majority in illiteracy and poverty so that the traditional cultural gap is perpetuated. This is why they are in favour of caste being the criterion to provide relief.

The basic fact which every citizen of India has to

acknowledge is that two thirds or more of the citizens of India are steeped in illiteracy and suffer utter poverty. Even the most advanced group in India, the Parsis, created a trust many decades ago to provide houses and pensions to the poor among them so that they do not go round bagging. It is a normal social phenomenon that about five to ten per cent of any group in any nation will need social welfare services. On the other hand, one of the glaring realities is that more advanced and politically well organized sections of the backward classes who manage to get all the benefits and they are the most vocal in their professions for the welfare of the backward sections of their cast or group. It is also well known that these backward sections of the caste make full use of the backwardness of their group to consolidate their own political power and to recruit well educated and well employed sons-in-law to their families.

The Backward Class Commission was appointed in 1953. Kaka Kalelkar was the chairman of the Commission. The commission was appointed according to Article 340 of the Indian constitution. The commission's main concern was to determine the criteria to be adopted to provide concessions to 'socially and educationally backward classes' (S.E.B.C) besides the scheduled castes and scheduled tribes. The commission was also incharge of preparing a list of such classes. At the beginning the commission found that while the various groups came forward to represent their condition as castes, no statistical information was available in this respect since the census of 1951 had not collected such information. This is one of the basic contradictions in the social life of the country. Since caste is a social fact such lists may be presumed to be made in terms of caste. But the constitution does not recognize caste, except the scheduled caste. The collection of castewise figures according to caste was given up because they were presumed to perpetuate caste distinctions, but caste-wise figures are necessary to provide them relief on the model scheduled caste. The commission prepared a list of about 2400 castes on the basis of the position of the caste in social hierarchy, percentage of literacy and its representation in Government service and in industries etc., taking as a basis the lists of other backward classes published by the Education Ministry and by the State Governments and also the representations made by several groups. The commission also revised lists of scheduled castes and scheduled tribes on the basis of the new information available. The commission noted that the great majority of the backward classes are ignorant, illiterate and poor. They are easily exploited by several classes of persons like the traders and the money lenders. It has also noted that the rigorous of caste system prevail and untouchability is being still practised in a pronounced manner in the rural areas. This has led to the formation of caste groups or combines in order to secure redress of their grievances; some of the representatives of the backward classes pleaded that though this trend is not healthy, it is inevitable to protect themselves. Another discrimination being practised in the rural areas is to prevent admission of their boys and girls to schools. Unless these social inequalities are removed, they can not have a fair deal.

The commission also noted that the administrative system it self, which was to implement the constitutional provisions, is tainted by casteism; this is one of the reasons why the backward classes have no confidence in securing a fair deal even from the administration. The commission also draws pointed attention to the contradiction between the theory and practice of Hinduism. While in theory Hinduism recognizes the concept of universality in practice it follows the laws of Manu which perpetuate the four fold division of the social order and the superiority of the Brahmin class. According to the terms of reference the commission was asked to consider whether any sections of the people, in addition to the scheduled castes and scheduled tribes should be treated as socially and educationally backward classes. Thus the words specifically used are classes and sections and not castes and yet as explained in the body of the report of the words sections and classes "can in the present context mean nothing but castes, and no other interpretation feasible. But castesim effects the solidarity of the nation. This is the basic dilemma, unless castes are noted remedial measures can not be implemented; if remedies are on caste basis, the solidarity of the nation will be seriously effected. It must be fully recognized that the backwardness of this large section of the people is based on their birth, they are treated as inferiors on account of their birth in a caste. There are many restraints on them particularly in the rural areas where eighty per cent of the people live and where social relations are based solely on the basis of caste. Even in the urban areas they are handicapped because of their dress, appearance and speech which reveal their poverty as well as illiteracy. In other words, their backwardness due to their social handicaps.

As already pointed out that fundamental rights are non-absolute by virtue of having supplementary qualifying provisions, it shall be essential to look at the restrictions hedged around the rights relating to equality. Article 15 (3) and (4) thus lay down that though there can be no discrimination between the parsons on several grounds, it shall be open for the State to make any provision for the welfare of women and children or for the advancement of socially and educationally backward classes of the society. Similarly, in case of Article 16 providing for non-discrimination in the matters of public employment, it is further said that the state can make special reservations and safeguards for the representation of the weaker sections of the society in public institutions or that it shall be open for the state to lay down qualifications of residence in respect of public employment in any part of the country.

Immediately after inauguration of the constitution, a

point of constitutional dispute arose in the Champakam Dorairajan case. The Supreme Court struck down an order of the Madras Government wherein reservation of seats in medical colleges was made in such a way that the backward classes could have a position of weightage at the time of seeking admissions. The court did not accept the argument of the Government that it was done to give effect to Article 46 of the constitution contained in part-IV of the directive principles of state policy. Thus, the first constitution amendment Act 1951 was made that empowered the state to make special arrangements for the socially and educationally backward classes of the society. Clause 4 was added to Article 15 and it says, "nothing in this Article or in clause (2) of Article 29 shall prevent the state from making any special provision for the advancement of any socially and educationally backward classes of citizens or for the scheduled castes and the scheduled tribes. Thus came into being what is known as, the law of protective discrimination in India. It may be asked as to what is the meaning of backward classes? Nowhere has this important term been defined in the constitution and it has been left to the state to explain it in a proper way. Caste can not be made the basis in this regard no matter it constitutes an important condition;nor can poverty be taken as the basis, nor can the factor of inadequate representation in the public services be given recognition for the purpose. What is needed is that social and educational circumstances should be kapt in mind while determining the category of backward classes. Moreover, any explanation of the state in this regard is subject to judicial review. As such, it lies with in the powers of the courts to see whether a classification made by the state or an explanation added thereto is reasonable or not. In case the court is not satisfied with the explanation of the state, it can strike down the explanation on the ground that it contravenes the sprit of Article 13 clause 2 of the constitution.

It is also needed that the provision of special reservation for backward classes should not cross the limit of reasonableness so that the deserving person of other classes are put to unnecessary disadvantage. That is, the area of special reservation for backward classes should be confined to the limits of reasonableness and it is for the courts to see as to what the 'scope of reasonableness' implies. For instance, as the court held, while the reservation of seats in the medical colleges of the State of Kerala for the Latin Christians, Muslims and Izhavas was well within the 'reasonable limits', it could not cover within its fold the case of the wards of the medical staff serving therein. Apart from this, it is also required that such special reservations made by the 'State' should be governed by the norm of 'impartiality'. The purpose behind them should not be to accord benefits to a particular class at the cost of others, or that such a step should not be taken owing to the pressure of some extraneous factors.

The case of protective or compensatory discrimination in our country should also be studied in the light of the fact that the makers of the Constitution had taken it well into their consideration. Dr. B.R. Ambedkar had so pointed out: "We must begin by acknowledging first that there is complete absence of two things in Indian society. One of them is inequality. On the social plane, we have in India a society based on privilege of graded inequality which means elevation for some and degradation for others. One the economic plane, we have a society in which there are some who have immense wealth as against the many who are living in abject poverty. On the 26th of January 1950, we are going to enter into a life of contradictions. In politics we have equality and in social and economic life we have inequality. We must remove this contradiction at the earliest possible moment, or else those who suffer from inequality will blow up the structure of political democracy which the Assembly has so laboriously built."

One more factor that violated the principle of 'ideal equality' is the incorporation of the qualification relating to long residence or domicile in matters of public employment. As the States Reorganization Act of 1956 vide its Sec. 29 gave recognition to the principle of 'domicile' in order to do away with certain political problems at the moment, an amendment of Art. 16 was made as a necessary consequence of the same. Thus, clause 3 was added to it. It says: "Nothing in this article shall prevent Parliament from making any law, prescribing, in regard to a class or classes of employment or appointment to an office.......any requirement as to residence within that State or Union Territory prior to such employment or appointment." It was done particularly for the benefit of the people living in the Telangana region of the newly born State of Andhra Pradesh who were thriving on certain benefits given to them by the Nizam of Hyderabad (vide his firman of 1919) for no other purpose than to counter the growing influence of the freedom movement in his princely state. Known as the Mulki Rules, the residential or domiciliary qualification became a clear violation of the right to equality as enshrined in the original Constitution.

The Supreme Court has laid down that 'equal protection means equal protection under equal circumstances.' In simple words, it means that the privileges of a legislator cannot be made equal to the privileges of a judge. An ordinary man cannot claim the amenities available to a high-ranking public servant. What it really means is that there can be no discrimination among people at the same level, or having the same status. The meaning of equality seems to have been carried to an extreme length when we find that the State can legitimately take to the course of making protective discrimination for the advancement of the weaker sections of the community. Thus, reservations and safeguards for the persons belonging to the Scheduled Castes and Scheduled Tribes do amount to the breach of the principle of the equality until we examine the whole case of our country from a sociological standpoint to justify the policy of protective discrimination. Herein lies a potential source of controversies emanating from the legislative enactment and their interpretations by the court.

There was nothing wrong with the principle of reservation. Without it the formidable task of removing the glaring disparities and social inequalities in our diverse society could not be accomplished. But what was, infact, meant to be a concession on the ground of economic upliftment has become a vote catching instrument at the hands of the ruling parties.

Few months after V.P. Singh took over as prime minister he faced the first most major combat in the anti-Mandal agitation. The National front in its election manifesto of 1989 supported substantial reservation in employment, education and public offices to Backward classes, observing at the same time that the recommendation of the Mandal commission will be implemented expeditiously.

On 7th August, 1990, V.P. Singh stunned the entire nation by announcing the government's acceptance of some recommendations of the Mandal Commission Report in parliament. He announced that a reservation of 27 % was to be made for the socially and educationally backward classes and that was to be applicable to the service under central Government and its public undertakings.

The Moraraji Desai Government in 1977 set up the Mandal Commission. But it is worth-noting that although Indira Gandhi summarily scrapped many of the recommendations of various commissions set up by Janata Party government, she did not outrightly reject the Mandal Report, nor did she take it up for consideration. Later, Rajiv Gandhi also did exactly the same thing. Why then after 10 years did the National Front make the Mandal Report a major plank of its election platform. It is being said by many an observer that V.P. Singh was indulging in cross populism to make a base for himself and thereby ensure his full tenure as the prime minister. But at the timing of its acceptance by the V.P. Singh government came as a complete surprise to all including even the MPs of ruling Janata Dal.

In the last week of August 1990 the stir was spreading far and wide. Whole India, was in the throes of frenzied violence. What began a mild-cat-protest? against V.P. Singh's reservation muddler later on transformed into an intense violence.

The question one has to ask is that why such type of caste politics was followed by a political leader and not in the past by any of his predecessors in his position? A most convincing of V.P. Singh's move on the Mandal Report was the Deputy Prime Minister Devilal's dismissal from the Government and his call for a mass rally on 9th August 1990, at the Boat Club at Delhi. In the rally Devi Lal was going to announce that V.P. Singh was not implementing the recommendations of Mandal Commission. This was the reason that Kanshi Ram, the leader of Bahujan Samaj Party attended the rally with Devi Lal. That was the first and last sitting of Kansi Ram with Devi Lal in a rally. Feeling politically insecure V.P. Singh was seriously planning to take the wind out of Devi Lal's sails. To countermine Devi Lal, V.P. Singh announced the implementation of some recommendations of the Mandal Commission. V.P. Singh calculated that Devi Lal would be deflected if he could be perceived as a champion of the backward communities.

No doubt, these events as a kerosene oil in a fire in terms of the implementation of some recommendations of Mandal commission report. But it does not matter much as to what impact the exist of Devi Lal had on this issue. It could have been delayed only by months and years and not by decades. There have been more stirring among these backward classes in recent years than in the past and they did play decisive role many in of the constituencies in north India in the last elections, for the Lok Sabha in 1989 and for the state Assemblies in early 1990. The MPs and MLAs belonging to the OBCs constitute a sizable section of the legislators. They wanted compliment this measure. So, it had to be done.

The identification of OBCs as attempted by the commission is somewhat confusing in the sense that the details about the data collected, the exact methodology followed and the final tables have not been made available by the commission. All that is made available is a list of the state-wise tables which were prepared. But the tables themselves have not been produced, nor has any detailed note on the manner in which the data collected through the survey, were used and published by the commission. Further, the commission hold that the method of socio-educational field survey was objective because the point system did not allow any subjective assessment. This method was found to be highly dependable in practice because as a result of its application most of the well known socially and educationally backward castes were identified as backward However, in some cases, the findings based on socio-educational field survey happened to be in consistent with the living social reality. For example, the social status of kasera caste in Bihar, Dhobi in Gujarat, Agasa in Karnataka, Kumbhar in Rajasthan, Badager in Tamilnadu etc. is known to be very low. Yet these castes scored below 11 points and this, qualified for ranking as forward.

Further, for identifying OBCs in the central government services the commission used two criteria for both Hindu and non-Hindu communities. In respect employees belonging to Hindu communities, the following criteria were adopted. First', an employer was deemed be socially backward if he does not belong to any of the three twice born varnas, i.e.

he is neither a Brahmin, nor a Kshatriya nor a Vaishya. Secondly, he was deemed to be educationally backward if neither his father nor his grand father had studied beyond the primary level.

As regard the non-Hindu communities (i) an employee was demand to be socially backward if either (a) he is a convert from those Hindu communities which have been defined as socially backward as in case of the Hindu communities above, or (b) in case he is not such a convert, his parental income is below the poverty line, i.e. Rs. 71 per head per month, (ii) he was deemed to be educationally backward if neither his father nor his grand father had studied beyond the primary level.

Here, it must be noted that an employee is qualified for membership of OBCs only if, both socially and educationally he was found to be backward according to the above criteria. Hence, the criteria that the Mandal commission has recommended reservation only on the basic of caste is not justified. In fact, it adopted, multiple approach, for the identification of OBCs for the purpose of reservation. The result is the inclusion of castes in the OBCs whose social and educational backwardness is not self – evident, and whose claim to economic backwardness arouses doubts. This is so about, say, the vokkaligas in Karnataka, the Yadavas and Kurmis in Bihar and Ahirs and Yadavas in U.P. As the study prepared by the Tata institute of social sciences, Mumbai for the commission had pointed out, the Vokkaligas are a dominant landed peasants and they employ labours mainly of OBCs and also belonging to the SCs and STs, on a large scale.

The inclusion of such castes as a whole in the OBC category for the purpose of special facilities such as reservation can not looked askance at. Further, enough indications exists of the very shady way in which the OBC lists have been prepared by the commission. Jats are treated as OBC for Ajmer in Rajasthan but not elsewhere. Dhobbies are in the list of the OBC in U.P, but not in Bihar. In Orissa, six scheduled castes and fourteen scheduled tribes have been shown as OBCs. In Maharashtra many kumbi sub-castes are shown as OBC, ignoring the increasing inclusion many of them in the over all Maratha caste which is treated as forward. All in all, there is sufficient material to show that reliance on the Mandal lists can not but give rise too much agitation, litigation and confusion in administration. It is also interesting to not that all the three technical experts, whose contribution to working out the methodology adopted by the commission has been acknowledged by it, have openly repudiated having had any association with the finalization of the findings and even the conduct and conclusion of the survey.

Prof. B.K. Roy Burman has stated that when the commission found that the findings of the pilot survey were not to its liking, they began to temper with the methodology and ignored the experts. The experts did not come to know whether they are survey design was used. Even the final tables were never shown to them. Similarly, Prof.. M.N. Srinivas and Prof. Yogendra Singh the other experts maintained in the report have clarified that they has almost nothing to do with the report as it was prepared. Another argument against the report is that the major benefits of preservations and other welfare measures for OBCs will be concerned by the more advanced section of the backward communities. The commission itself accepted the view.

As soon as the V.P. Singh Government announced its decision to implement some recommendations of the Mandal Commission report, the nation took some time to realize the far reaching implications of the announcement.

When the reaction came, it was on an unprecedented scale. The subsequent events broadly followed to paths.

One was mounting demand for extension of similar facilities to other uncovered groups in society and the governments increasing readiness also to accommodate them. The second was the emergence of a firmer and determined resistance to the Mandal recommendations, viewing the Mandal report as various capable of planning Indian society in to a perpetual caste war.

Who took what side in the ideological battle? First, those who opposed the Mandal Commission were invariably the high caste Brahmins, Kshatriyas, Christians etc. Second, a few of the high caste Brahmins, kshatriyas, mostly in the left or associated with mass struggle, are supporting the Mandal Commission or remaining neutral. Third, there was a group of castes who were confused because they could potentially be included in the castes listed in the Mandal Commission but they were not included. Therefore, they could have two caste strategies, to oppose Mandal or to argue for inclusion. To oppose it aligned them with Brahmins and kshatriya, to argue for inclusion it aligned them with the Dalit-sudra castes. Fourth, Dalits and adivasis supported the Mandal Commission and were even ready to support widening its terms of reference, in spite of the fact that the Mandal Commission did not immediately benefit them, and in spite of the fact that twice born were using the name of Dalits and the truly backward to oppose the Mandal Commission on the grounds that it was extending reservations to economically advanced rural dominant castes who were the once responsible for committing atrocities on Dalits. The Dalits were also taking this stand on the basis of a caste strategy. That is they were quite aware that twice born opposition was not simply to 'OBC' reservations but to any kind of reservations, and that if they succeed in beating back the Sudras on this, they would next move to push back the Dalilts.

The protest was scattered throughout the country. There was some minor stir in the various southern states but it was more for the sake of form than anything else. It was in the northern states that the situation was sought to be catalyzed into a mass upsurge. The capital city Delhi after the student community took to the streets, had been transformed into a city of Bandhs and rallies. The administration closed all schools and colleges for a month. The Delhi transport corporation ordered the removal of glass panes from all its buses. Though the student groups showed good sense in persuading the protests to abandon the casteist slogans raised during the initial anti-Mandal hysteria, Sarad Yadav and Ram Vilas Paswan continued exhorting the backwards to come out into the streets for a numerical show down with anti-reservationists.

In Bihar though, Laloo Prasad Yadav was one of the chief minister who stand to gain the most from the implementation of the commission report, yet his state had witnessed some of the bloodiest anti-Mandal protests which claimed several lives. The reason is not difficult to spot. There are the backwards and there are the forwards among the backwards — like Yadavs, Kurmis and Keories – who have gained both economic and political power over the years like the Bhumihars, Brahmins and Rajputs. The upper castes in Bihar was so angry that an organisation called the "Rastriya Swarna Mukti Morcha" had been set up in Bhumihar dominated Muzarfarpur District to demand a separate 'Swarna Rajya' comprising areas in Bihar, Uttar Pradesh, Madhya Pradesh, West Bengal and Haryana.

Five months after Biju Pattanaik took over as Chief Minister he faced the fast major combat in the anti-Mandal agitation. He could have never foreseen the catastrophe just as he did not belief in caste politics. Orissa which is otherwise a tranquil state, was in the throes of a frenzied violence. Within few days nine people lost their lives. The fury fast started in the prestigious B.J.B. College of Bhubaneswar. Soon it spread to all other small places like Balugaon and Nirakarpur. In an unprecedented swoop, the violent mob almost killed an officer in charge of Balugan Police Station. In Cuttack the Mandal agitation witnessed the glory death of Alok Mahapatra, the general secretary of the National Student's Union of India. Biju Pattanaik did not need V.P. Singh's help to create a vote Bank. He had not merely decided against implementing the report but also came out publicly against caste based reservations. But the violence continued even after the Chief Minister's announcement. The movement he disassociated himself from the trickery that was the Mandal Commission, the central leaders of the Janata Dal took umbrage against Biju. They demanded Biju Pattanaik's head for deriding party politics.

Ironical as it may seen, Biju Pattanaik who initially showed reluctance to the reservations was months later soon holding a National convention of the Janata Dal in Puri, where the reservation issue was ratified overwhelmingly. Social justice had now come to occupy the centre stage. Three years later, on September 10th, 1993 he announced reserving 12 % of vacancies for the socially and educationally backward classes in all recruitment in his state.

In Uttar Pradesh, Mulayam Singh Yadav had fewer trouble. Though the anti Mandal agitation has claimed lives, but it had less potential for an all out war. In Punjab students managed to paralyze normal life. Chief Minister Hukum Singh announced that he would leave it to a popular Government to decide on implementing the report because the various Akali and Militant groups seemed unable to take a stand on the issue. Haryana witnessed far more trouble possibly because the State Government was not exactly averse to fomenting it. Chief Minister Om Prakesh Choutala welcomed the implementation of Mandal Commission report but then in obvious an attempt to embarrass the union Government, appointed a backward commission. He claimed to had done so because deputations of many communities including Jats, Jat-Sikhs, Ahirs, Gujjars, Sainis, Rodes and Moors, had complained that despite being socially and educationally backward, they had not been included in the list of beneficiaries.

Himachal Pradesh's BJP chief minister Santa Kumar rejected the report outright and announced that the Government proposed to implement the Antodaya Scheme instead, by which one lakh poor families will be chosen for benefits. The army had to be called out in half a dozen towns as clashes between pro and anti-reservationists go out of hand.

Gujarat remained peaceful this time. It was largely due to the shrewd handling of the situation by chief minister Chimanbhai Patel. He announced that the state would not implement the commission's recommendations. While the rest of the south remained peaceful, Congress (I) ruled Andhra Pradesh had its share of rail and rasta rokos, protest rallies and bandhs.

Suddenly, unexpected alliances and equations had emerged, as leaders struggle to juggle electoral politics with caste affiliations and party ideologies and politics. Thus, Mandal Commission Report had split the political parties along caste lines. The Janata Dal being the major political party in the front was totally responsible for the implementation of some recommendations of Mandal Commission. The report had polarized political forces even within the ruling National Front. Orissa chief minister Biju Patnaik raised the first standard of revolt angrily accusing the Prime Minister of inciting caste violence. Until he spoke out, patnaik was among Singh's staunchest supporters. So when his statement was splashed countrywide a sense of doom gripped the party. But when more than a dozen MPs from Orissa called on V.P. Singh and told him they were opposed to Biju Patnaik's out burst, Biju Patnaik sensed and incipient revolt in his own house and within twenty four hours had softened his own stand. Chandra Sekhar, Yaswant Singh and Harmohan Dhawan condemned the Mandal move publicly. Both L.K. Advani and Atal Behari Bajpayee almost threatened to with draw their support if the government did not review its stand, yet they failed to come out with a clear thesis against the reservations. While the student leaders of Congress (I) protested in Delhi, the party maintained a cryptic silence. Rajiv Gandhi brought a resolution drafted by Mani Sankar Aiyer, which closely advocated the total rejection of the Mandal report. However, no sooner did the meeting began than the party stood clearly divided along caste and class lines. Vasant Sathe, a Brahmin, attacked the report declaring, V.P. Singh is reviving the caste system. The party must fight it. Only to come up against an aggressive array of backward class leaders like B. Shankaranand, Sita Ram Kesri, P. Shiv Shankar, D.P. Yadav and Margatham Chandrashekhar, countered, "the congress has always fought for the downtrodden. How can we oppose the Mandal Report now"? Rajiv Gandhi was forced to reach for a compromise.

The left parties were almost vertically divided on this issue. The CPI was the first to come out in defense of the reservations for the backward classes. The CPI (M) which has all along been against reservation on the caste basis and particularly, against reservation for the backward classes found itself forced to support the V.P. Singh government's decision to implement reservation for the OBCs. While the West Bengal clique was against, the Kerala group was for Mandal. The CPI (M) had consistently maintained that there should be an economic criterion for reservations. A week later the politburo modified this general stand for an economic criterion to one of an economic criterion for the Backward classes. It maintained that with in the reservation allotted backward classes there should be an economic criterion. If the CPI (M) exhibits a kind of bowing to political compulsions, the CPI-ML exhibits exactly the opposite kind of bowing to its political compulsions.

At last a special nine-judge Bench of the Supreme Court by a majority-judgement by upholding the 27 per cent reservation for backward classes has enunciated for reaching principles about the scope of Article 16 (4) of our constitution. After the judgement, there had been several positive developments on the reservation and social justice front. A broad consensus had emerged at the national level on reservation policy, its scope and priorities as well as its constitutional limits. The Janata Dal's pre-eminent leader, V.P. Singh, Laloo Prasad Yadav, Mulayam Singh and several other figures in the third formation are strongly identified by the masses as champions of social Justice.

The issue behind the clash of interests on reservation is deep going and basic to the Indian social order. Why is it that reservation, or compensatory discrimination, is such a hot potato? Why does it divide young people so fiercely socially, emotionally and ideologically?

At one level, the effects of reservation are tremendously exaggerated and magnified to generate strong passions among the non-beneficiaries. A lesson must be learnt from the experience of the anti-Mandal Movement. The experience of SCs and STs on the one hand and the OBCs on the other must be differentiated and the differences kept in focus, but the experience of both categories relates to a society that scholars have characterized as uniquely unequal, as the land of an inviolable organization by birth. Caste, which exemplifies social oppression, inequality and injustice in a way that detracts profoundly from the achievement of Indian civilization over the ages, has shown a surprising durability and resilience in the face of socio – economic, political and cultural change and the forces of modernization. The task of building a secular, democratic society constantly interacts with this issue. It is not just communalism which threatens secularism and democracy. Caste divisions, prejudices and hierarchy militate against the idea that we have a secular, democratic society in place.

Reservation redefined again on November 19, 1999 when the central Government expended the list of backward classes and added 126 more sub-castes from 17 States of the Indian Union. The decision was taken in the meeting of the union cabinet in which, it approved the recommendations of the national backward castes commission. This was the second amendment in the list of backward castes in two months. Some sub-castes, which were included in the list are Yadavs, Kasais, Telis, Sahus, Teli Rathods, Ram Garahias, Julahs, Sainis, Swarnakaras, Sukariars, Shersha Badis etc. These sub castes belongs to the States of Uttar Pradesh, Andhra Pradesh, Bihar, Goa, Chandigarh, Kerala, Madhya Pradesh, Rajasthan, Karnataka, Gujarat, Orissa, Tripura, Tamil Nadu, West Bengal, Pondicherry and Sikkim. Most of the backward sub-castes have been included from Uttar Pradesh. This step of the Government has given a new fillip to the reservation issue. Clearly, the B.J.P Government in the center planed to extend its mass base that was always in favour of the Government's and political ideologies promoted by the Congress party. This decision has a political things as the N.D.A. led coalition Government was like to be on its own and hence it would like to make deep in roads into the vote banks of backward sub-castes by pleasing them.

In the Lok Sabha reservation of backward castes would continue for a period of ten years, starting from the day of January 2000. It is our sanguine that reservations could not cease even after January 26, 2000, a new legislation passed in the Lok Sabha in order to extend reservation in the Lok Sabha even after stipulated date. It is an irony that the backwardness of a man is so vital for the survival of all the political groups. Hence, these groups tries to extend 'favours" to them in order to keep their sailing. This honour is, perhaps, too much for the common man belonging to a scheduled sub-caste, whose value is nothing more then the vote that he is required to cast at the hustling.

On the eve of the elections of the 13th Lok Sabha the Jat Mahasabha had announced the withdrawal of its support to the Congress as it had failed to secure reservation for Jats. The B.J.P took the opportunity to secure reservation for the Jats. Rajputs did not react kindly to this move. Muslims and Christians also demanded reservation. The Samajvadi Party the Bahujana Samaja Party and Congress supported Muslim on the issue of reservation. B.J.P. supported array of sub-castes for their inclusion in the coveted list and these were mainly Hindus and Sikhs. Therefore, all the parties have priorities in terms of reservation of caste as well. The B.J.P. supported the "Jat cause" and reaped rich benefits. Mr. Sahib Singh Verma the ousted C.M. of Delhi was elected as a M.P. in 13th Lok Sabha. The areas of outer Delhi as is well known are Jat strong holds. The B.J.P. out performed all other parties in these areas and was way ahead of others.

Article 16 of the constitution assures job reservations for any backward class, which has not been adequately represented in the services under the state in question. Clause 1 of the this article states, " there shall be equality of opportunity for all citizens in matters relating to employment or to appointment to any office under the State. These two views were in contradiction with each other. Hence, the Supreme Court ruled in 1992 that the power of reservation under Article 16 ought to be exercised in a fair manner and within reasonable limits. The two provisions, stated above, are complementary, provided that both are given equal importance without giving lower weightage to the other. The Supreme Court discussed the contradiction with each other and the issue being complementary with each other. The Court had remarked, in the context of the *Indira Sawhney versus the Union of India* case that large segments of population enjoying political advantages could use their backward status. Therefore, these castes could gain in terms of economic benefits, issue of land and employment in the PSUs. The Government was advised not to give reservation to these castes. The Supreme Court had also stated that backwardness under clause 4 of article 16 only meant social backwardness and the backward classes of citizens were those who had low social standing in the society and whose occupations as well income levels were low.

The upper limit of reservation also kept at 50 % through judicial rulings. The judiciary fears that excessive reservation is likely to lead to reduced number of opportunities for man of merit in those categories that are not reserved. The supreme court had advised the Government that in the fields of medicine, engineering, nuclear research, aviation, research and development and other specialty areas, reservation of any type was not advisable; the highly technical nature of these jobs demanded only those candidates who possessed the skills to perform the specific tasks. The court had opined that there would always be those candidates who would be able to qualify in the open competitions due to their merits and toil, for admission to super specialty courses. And this could be done without lowering the admission criteria for these candidates. In sum, if a candidate belonged to a backward caste, he could still become an engineer or a doctor, depending upon the hard work put in by him to achieve his goal. There is supposed to be a competition of the brains and not of the various castes and sub-castes, as is being done at present.

But the rulings of the Supreme Court have not been understood in the right perspective by any Government; which has ruled in the center. The 77th Amendment of 1995 had restored reservation in support of scheduled castes and scheduled tribes employees, it was disallowed in the Indira Sawhney case. This was effected by inserting a new enabling provision (clause 4–A) in Article 16 of Indian constitution. This clause seems to promote the interest of those backward castes who enjoy political clout in the center as well as in the states. The latest amendments increase the reservation to more then the level of 50%. Thus the concept of creamy layer has been eliminated, which debars the forward sections of the backward castes from the benefits of reservation. This move would hurt the candidates of the general category. The real objective of reservation was to help the backward castes come out of the darkness of the social and economic backwardness. It was not meant to punish the meritorious candidates of the general category. If the thrust on reservation continues unabated, the problem of brain drain would assume serious proportions. The talented candidates of general category are already heading towards the west in search of greener pastures.

Further, within the same caste there could be a dangerous formation subgroups—backwards, more backwards and most backwards. The criterion for judgement would not be clear to any non Government organization, state run institution or judiciary. This would lead to intra castes conflicts. Inter caste conflicts would also rise in terms of number and intensity as the members of every caste would like their caste to be included for reservations in the Lok Sabha. State assemblies and educational institutions.

In order to curb the reservation menace, strict laws should be passed, which should be able to give reservation quotas to the candidates on the basis of economic backwardness. The criteria of social backwardness and religion ought to be done away with. As on date, the middle class people has been suffering on account of reservations. The middle class of Indian society has now become too powerful to be ignored. A reprisal from this group could be predicated in the year 2010 when the reservation issue in the Lok Sabha would be discussed again. Before that happens, the state must shift the criterion of reservation to economically backward groups. All the lists for jobs, educational and financial aid should be bifurcated according to the economic categories described earlier. This step could save India from a catastrophe that might lead to a grave crisis in the year 2010 A.D.

Both the reservation system and the policy of reservation have come under strong criticism. The use of caste groups to identify the beneficiaries of compensatory discrimination is responsible for perpetuating the caste system, accentuating caste consciousness and injecting caste into politics. Caste based reservation is against the basic sprit of the Indian constitution which promises the right to equality. This system is also inimical to merit because it enables incompetent to sneak from behind and deprive brilliant and deserving youth of college seats and jobs, thus destroying the nation's prospects of achieving greatness. The majority of people who take advantage of these reservations on the basis of birth are those who are already affluent. They only monopolize the benefits of reservations while the rest of the members of the caste or tribe remain exactly where they were.

The caste based policy of reservation, with all its criticism, has enough to comment in its favour. These castes are, by and large, yet to catch up with other castes notwithstanding all that the Government has done for them. It is common knowledge that caste being a fundamental reality of Indian society and a terrifying force of stability, the strategy of social action for changing our social system must be caste based. The policy of reservation is a preparation for bigger social change in the country which can not be accomplished unless a cultural revolution succeeds prior to that. Thus the policy of reservation is one of the weapons to fight against the evils of casteism rather then a plan to improve economic condition of scheduled castes and scheduled tribes and other backward classes.

It was called a watershed in post-independent India's history. Prime Minister Vishwanath Pratap Singh's decision in 1990 to implement the Mandal Commission recommendations was hailed and reviled with equal farvour. While the upper castes, especially Brahmins, saw it as the death knell of their aspirations, the backward castes and Dalits believed it was the gateway to a brave new world, free of Brahmincal hegemony. Upper caste students demonstrated noisily, immolated themselves in protest, but in vein. Four years later, after an injunction against it was removed following a historic Supreme Court verdict, the Mandal recommendations entered the statute books.

But 12 years after the announcement – and eight since the judgment both Brahmin fears and backward caste hopes appear to have been belied. Be it in national or north Indian politics, the bureaucracy or elsewhere, Brahmins are far from marginalised Nine of the 12 years have seen Brahmin Prime Ministers at the helm (P.V. Narasimha Rao and Atal Bihari Vajpayee); for five years there was also a Brahmin President (Sankar Dayal Sharma). The Lok Sabha Speaker Manohar Joshi was a Brahmin as were the Chief Ministers of many states.

The Brahmin roll call among top civil servants is even more impressive: National Security Adviser Brajesh Mishra, Cabinet Secretary Kamal Pande, Home Secretary N. Gopalaswamy, Finance Secretary S. Narayanan and Central Vigilance Commissioner P. Shanker were the leading lights among two dozen Brahmin secretaries at the Center. The chiefs of the Army and the Airforce, Gen. S. Padmanabhan and Air Chief Marshal S. Krishnswamy were Brahmins. Brahmins proliferating in top corporate positions, or straddling the heights of the culture and entertainment worlds are too many to name. Why, four permanent fixtures in the Indian cricket team—Sourav Ganguly, Sachin Tendulkar, Rahul Dravid and Anil Kumble—are Brahmins!.

The Brahmin domination of Hindu society goes back a long, long way. The Purusasukta legend—claiming the Brahmin emerged from the head of Purusa, the Primeval being, while the Kshatriya came out of Purusa's shoulders, the Vaishya from his thighs and the Shudra from his feet – first mentioned in the rig Veda, aptly symbolises the unquestioned sway the Brahmin has held for millennia. But in the twentieth century there occurred a curious, sweeping, worldwide reversal of long-cherished values: suddenly elitism — like empire and patriarchy — became a dirty word.

In the first half of the century the scheduled castes asserted themselves under Babasaheb Ambedkar, in south India, particularly Tamil Nadu, the backward castes rallied behind 'Periyar' E.V. Ramaswami Naicker. Half a century later, with the Mandal announcement, the backward upsurge reached north India.

Simultaneously, Kanshi Ram's Bahujan Samaj Party (BSP), slowly and painstakingly accreting support for years, suddenly grew wings in Uttar Pradesh, giving the scheduled castes-now renamed Dalits-a voice they had never before had. And as the anti-Mandal agitation failed, as the anti-upper caste, anti-Brahmin rhetoric of the BSP- and to a lesser degree, of the Samajawadi Party (SP) and the Rashtriya Janata Dal (RJD)—grew shriller, it was believed by many that the Brahmin had his day. "The upper castes did feel besieged," said Yogendra Yadav, political scientist and psephologist.

In south India, undoubtedly, lasting changes did occur, rendering Brahmins irrelevant in politics. In the bureaucracy, too, Brahmins have been reduced to a minority, but even that minority—as the list of top bureaucrats reveals—is not doing all that badly. Besides, south Indian Brahmins continue to thrive in the private sector, in the arts and related areas, in new fields of technology: the Indian contribution to software development, feted worldwide, is primarily the achievement of south Indian Brahmins.

In the north, Brahmins have held their own even more successfully. In the Hindi belt they still matter in politics, they still dominate the bureaucracy, they still possess sizeable land and economic resources. Indeed, it is their opponents' fire which has dimmed; the anti-Brahmin sloganeering of the nineties is no longer heard. Even Kanshi Ram and Mayawati now explicitly seek votes not just from the 'Bahujan Samaj' but from all sections of society, including the upper castes. Said sociologist Dhirubhai Sheth of the Center for the Study of Developing Societies: "Brahmins have shown an unexpected degree of resilience."

How did the Brahmin become so powerful in the first place? Recent research on caste questions if they were in fact, all that important. The central thesis of Dipankar Gupta's interrogating Caste, for instance, is that there was no single caste hierarchy, which was universally acknowledged and accepted by everyone in the caste system. "Every caste has always considered itself superior to every other caste," said Gupta, who teaches sociology at Jawaharlal Nehru University, Delhi. "But the poor castes, lacking wealth and power never dared to openly say so."

Gupta maintained that only those Brahmins who had plenty of wealth and land were dominant. "The Brahmins who were simply pujaris were not particularly revered," he said. The notion of unchallenged Brahmin superiority in ancient and medieval times, suggested Gupta, was a construct of the British. "When they took over the country they wanted to understand and codify the Indian caste system. They turned to the Brahmins, among the few literate groups then, for information. The Brahmins naturally gave them only their own point of view."

Whatever their position in the distant past, there is no doubt that Brahmins reached the zenith of their prestige under British rule. "The British needed a class of scribes to man their lower bureaucratic positions," said Gupta. "In those days the only literate castes were the Brahmins and Kayasthas, and these were the ones the British recruited. These salaried positions gave the Brahmins extraordinary power over Indian society."

Naturally, other castes, equally wealthy but not so well-read, resented this dominance. Even so, Brahmins may not have attracted so much opprobrium had they not carried their phobia of 'pollution' to extreme lengths. As notions of democracy and human equality spread, the inexcusable practice of untouchability towards the Dalits, the unwillingness to dine with other castes considered lowly, evoked an enormous backlash. Ambedkar led the battle for the Dalits; Periyar raised the banner of backward caste revolt in Tamil Nadu. "The castes which backed Periyar were hardly the wretched of the earth," said Gupta. "They were rich, powerful castes, unwilling to stomach Brahmin superiority."

The coming of Independence, and universal suffrage with it, irreversibly weakened the Brahmin's position. Suddenly this caste had to confront the fact that, for all its influence, its numbers were few: even in Uttar Pradesh, where Brahmins are most numerous, they constitute just 9 per cent. In Tamil Nadu they form less than 3 per cent. When the DMK, an offshoot of Periyar's Dravida Kazagham (DK) won power in 1967, the writing for Brahmins was on the wall. "Once the DMK took charge it embarked on a severe and systematic programme of reverse discrimination," said Sheth. "Reservation quotas were raised to such high levels that Brahmins were squeezed out of government-owned educational institutions and jobs."

"In the south, caste battles were polarised between Brahmins and non-Brahmins." said Sheth. "In north India, not only were Brahmins more numerous, but there were also other upper castes with whom they could ally." Besides, added Gupta the Jajmani system of village economy lasted longer in the north than in the south. "As long as it existed the power and influence of the landed Brahmin remained. But now that has collapsed in the north as well."

"The main reason Brahmins, especially in north India were able to preserve their position despite the coming of democracy," said Satish Deshpande of the Institute of Economic Growth, "was the peculiar naivete and optimism of the Nehruvian era. At the time it was thought that as the country progressed, caste would just wither away. But in fact this approach only led to the perpetuation of inequality. A caste –blind polity also remained blind to the persistence of caste dominance."

But not for ever, Thanks to reservations and reforms, there has been the rise of a substantial middle class among the scheduled castes and tribes; the Green Revolution of the sixties empowered sections of the backward castes; and finally, V.P Singh's fateful decision led to the backward and Dalit assertion of the early 90s. As the frenzy of the anti-Mandal agitation showed, pure panic set in among the upper castes, especially Brahmins.

Yet the deluge never came. The Brahmins of north India have not been washed away. How did they stave off the backward class-Dalit threat? Politically, their sizeable numbers proved crucial. At 9 per cent, Brahmins are the largest caste in Uttar Pradesh after Jadavs (12 per cent). As castes like the Jats and the Yadavs have repeatedly proved, determined minorities can, in the electoral arena, aided by wealth, weapons and proper organisation, overcome the handicap of moderate numbers. Brahmins, too, have not shied away form using strong-arm methods to enforce their electoral will in the past, but defensive after the Mandal upheaval they have lately restricted themselves, like the Muslims, to care full tactical voting.

"Across much of north India, Brahmins have joined forces with castes like Rajputs and Banias to form broadband upper caste coalitions," said Sheth. "This is a recent development. In the past, before the backward classes became politically conscious, these upper castes, especially Brahmins and Thakurs, were the main rivals for state power." Such a coalition so augments their numbers that no political party can ignore them. But the upper castes have done more. "They have been very clever at exploiting the political and regional fragmentation of the backward castes to their advantage," observed Yogendra Yadav.

Dalit intellectuals, mostly city-based, continue to rail against Brahmanvad," said Dalit intellectual Chandrabhan Prasad. " That is because they are in Government service, or their Dalit friends are, and often suffer minor humiliations at the hands of upper caste officers, especially Brahmins. But the bulk of Dalits in the villages has realised that the main enemies of Dalits are not Brahmins. Their real oppressors are the intermediate and elite backward castes, who are the powerful landowners today." Agreed Sheth: "That is why an upper caste-Dalit coalition, though unstable, is at least possible, as we have seen in UP. It is proving more tenable than a backward-Dalit coalition."

Beyond politics, in the professional world, the Brahmin's main survival weapon has been their legacy of education. " Earlier Brahmins had status power," said Sheth. "Now that has gone. But the benefits they obtained on account of that status in the past the education they received down several generation, in some cases vast amount of land and money they came to possess — remain with them still."

What of the future? Brahmins may have held out so far, but they were far from optimistic. "It is still early years for the Mandal entrants," said a top BJP politician. "Ten years from now the upper castes will be finished in the north Indian bureaucracy as well." As soon as their confidence is won, upper caste bureaucrats embark on stories about the inefficiency and venality of backward caste and Dalit officers. "In coming years efficiency will plummet, the country will suffer terribly. I'm trying to send my children abroad," said a Brahmin joint secretary.

"Anti-reservation feeling is much stronger now among the upper castes than in the past," said Yogendra Yadav. "Some of the horror stories of poor performance may be true," admitted Dipankar Gupta. "But the other castes are also learning fast. The second generation of educated backwards and Dalits will be much more capable than the first."

Of course, there is always the private sector. As long as reservation remain confined to state-owned services, Brahmins can rejoice: for the private sector is expanding, while the state sector is shrinking. It may be mere coincidence, but the move away from increasing state control began in 1991, one year after the Mandal agitation. As second generation and third generation economic reforms follow, as more and more areas are privatised and more and more PSUs disinvested. Brahmin hegemony is likely to get a fresh lease of life. By the time the backwards and Dalits get to rule the state empire, they may find, like the later Mughal emperors, that there is little of the empire left to rule.

A Magna Carta, a Mandal Commission for Dalits or just another well-intentioned attempt distends to be mired in crossfire of vested interests? In March 2005 without much fanfare, the UPA regime constituted a high-level committee of 12 Union ministers and the deputy chairman of the Planning Commission to prepare an action plan "identifying the gaps in existing schemes" for Dalits. A 33-point agenda has also been laid down. If the panel is serious, this could mean radical changes in the way Dalits live.

The ambitious "remit" (area of authority) includes land distribution, reservation in private educational institutions including technical and professional institutes, filling up of the back log in reserved jobs, strict implementation of the scholarship policy, funds allocation for Dalit welfare programmes, a law to ensure state Assemblies and Parliament debate the Scheduled Caste commission reports and much more.

Good as it sounds on paper, will the panel be able to deliver? D. Raja, CPI secretary and the lone Dalit among Left leaders, says, "Not much was done to give the Dalits their due share in wealth creation and distribution. So there's a growing agitation among them that the government can't wish away. This has compelled the latter to address certain serious issues. Let us see how serious their efforts are"

Professor S.K. Thorat, director, Indian Institute of Dalit Studies, feels the constitution of the panel and its agenda point towards a growing recognition that Dalit welfare programmes have not worked on the ground. "This document (the 33-point agenda) has the potential of being radical if the assertions on land distribution and reservation in private educational institutes translate into action," says Thorat.

Despite the many promises and legislation, only 18 lakh acres of land were distributed in the last 50 years. And 20 per cent of this happened in Left-ruled West Bengal. Apart from the feudal caste order that alienated Dalits form the land they tilled, there were laws like the Punjab Land Alienation Act of 1901 that made it impossible for

Dalits to own land. As a result, 94 per cent Dalits farm workers in Punjab do not own land. All over India, 62 per cent of the rural Dalit population are landless, casual farm labour.

The most immediate and pressing demand is for filling up existing reserved jobs. For instance, Delhi University – its affiliated colleges have 7,000 teachers-has just 200 from the SC/ST community when the government quota mandates over 1,500. Another major area of concern is school dropouts. While enrolment levels of Dalit students is as good as that in the rest of society, the dropout ratio is very high, 76 per cent till 10th standard and around 90 per cent at the 12th standard level. The reason: obviously poverty.

The document though is silent on a radical idea mooted by Dalit bureaucrats and intellectuals – giving a portion of government contracts to Dalits. Still the Congress thinking is that filling up back log vacancies and ensuring education for their children would help it regain some credibility among the Dalit masses.

12

Casteism in States of India

In Indian politics, caste plays a vital role as the political behaviour of the mass is often influenced by caste consideration. Caste plays a major role in the state and local politics, but it plays only a marginal role at the all India level. Further, at state level also it plays different roles in different states. Andre Beteille aptly said, "caste enters much more directly into the composition of political elites at state level". Particularly in the States of Andhra Pradesh, Bihar, Haryana, Karnakata, Kerala, Maharastra, Tamil Nadu and Uttar Pradesh caste has been a major and dominant factor of state politics in India.

The caste factor is so strong a factor in Andhra Pradesh that all the political parties, national and regional, communist and non-communist formulate their politics, programmes and activities without reference to caste factor. The electoral politics in Andhra Pradesh is virtually caste politics. The Reddis, Kammas and Velamas constitute the three angles of Andhra's political triangle. The history of development of political parties in Andhra Pradesh can be legitimately described as a history of competition between Reddis and Kammas. At one time the delta region of state and railgene were referred as "Kamma Rastra" and "Reddi Seema." In elections the chances of success or failure of a candidate always depend upon his caste affiliations and his ability to use the caste factor for considering his support base and for dividing his opponents support base. Even regionalism with in Andhra stands based upon caste factor. The Telangana issue has been a caste issue in disguise. In the words of Srinivas, "The regional claims in Andhra are often only a disguise for caste claims." Thus, a peculiar thing about the caste politics in Andhra Pradesh is that, it always linked with the regional politics. The people of a particular caste living in a particular region have given a caste cum-regional complexion to the issues facing the state. In reality, the politics of Andhra Pradesh is dominated by triangular fight among the Reedi, Kamma and Velama communities.

The 1989 election was the first real reverse in N.T. Rama Rao's life. Caste factor was the important reason for the debacle of N.T. Rama Rao and his Telugu Desam Party in the elections of 1989. N.T. Rama Rao antagonized powerful and dominant castes & communities by his decision to abolish the village posts of Karnam and munsiff in the Andhra region and those of Patel and Patwari in the Telengana region, and his decision to abolish the hereditary rights of temple archakas and temple trustees. These decisions had made him unpopular in two ways; on the one side, these communities turned hostile because of loss of jobs. The other section of society that welcomed these measures was sore over the N.T. Rama Rao government's failure to usher in the alternative set up of village assistants because of endless litigation.

Tough there was no communal strife during his regime, a number of caste clashes occurred resulting in large scale violence and killings. He could contain communal tension in perennially sensitive Hyderabad, but failed to curb gang sterism in coastal Andhra districts. The rout of Telugu Desam in coastal Andhra was Partly due to caste riots which had made the entire Kapu community rise against the party.

That factionalism is almost endemic to congress party

affairs has been well documented among others by Myron, Weiner, Rajani Kothari, Paul Brass, Richard Sission and Stanly Cochanek. What should surprise however, is the fact that even a regional Party like the T.D.P was not free from this feature was quite evident from what preceded and followed the selection of its nominees to contest in the elections.

A close look on the study of Dr D. Suran Naidu, at the caste composition of party nominees of 8th and 9th Assembly elections in the constituencies of Srikakulam district, shows a slight shift in favour of the Kapu and Kalingi castes.

Comparison of the Caste of the T.D.P Candidates of 1985 and 1989 Assembly Elections

Caste	*1985*	*1989*
Velema	3	2
Kapu	2	3
Kalingi	1	3
Kamma	1	1
SC	2	2
ST.	1	1
Sri saina	1	—
Adi-Velama	1	—
	12	12

Source: Peoples' Mandate, 914, Sadashiv Peth, Pune.

From the above table it is clear that in the absence of an electoral wave working in its favour, the Telugu Desam Party was complied to take caste arithmetics more seriously in selecting its nominees. As against 3 Velama, 2 Kapu and 1 each representing Kalingi, Kamma, Srisaina and Adivelama communities in the previous election the party had nominated only members of locally dominant castes for all but one general seat. The party had nominated 3 each from Kapu and Kalingi caste, 2 belonging to velama community. Considerations on the basis of caste and faction had a similar role in the selection of Congress party nominee.

The politics of Bihar can be explained primarily in terms of caste. The caste consideration remains the main plank of all the parties, national or regional during elections, their profession to the contrary notwithstanding. One of the poorest state in India, caste factor always predominates the struggle for power in Bihar Politics. Rajputs, Brahmins, Kayasthas and Adivasis constitute the four caste segments of Bihar Politics. The Rajputs and Brahmins, by virtue of their superior economic position and social status have been dominating Bihar politics.

It is unfortunate that the persecution of lower caste groups by members of some of the upper and middle castes seems to have intensified. Parliament was told by Government on December 5, 1987 that 14012 cases of atrocities on the Harijans and 1829 of Girijans had been reported between September 1986 and October 1987. Reports of such atrocities come in form of almost all States, though Bihar earned notoriety because of the brutal attacks on low caste labourers in Belchi, Bajitpur and Pipra. If the statistics of conflicts and caste riots in Bihar are carefully examined, the incidence of violence shows some definite patterns. In the incidents Bajitpur, Khajuria and some other places the main issue were wage, share croppers' rights, over their cultivated land and possession of Government distributed land. In Belchi and to a certain extent, in Bishrampur, fight was against social oppression, including sexual exploitation. The caste components of attackers were varied. In Bajitpur and pipra, they were Bhumihars, a particularly aggressive upper caste. In Bishramapur and Belchi, they were kurmis, a counterpoise to Bhumihars among backward castes. Whether Bhumihars or Yadavas and Kurmis, they were landlords who were determined to preserve their land.

Members of untouchable communities seeking a better economic and social deal have been subjected to harassment, beating, burning of homes and even murder. By far more startling in this context is the fact that Harijans in Bihar have turned increasingly militant and joined Naxalite organizations like the Indian peoples front to turn tables on the Thakurs.

Since its division in 1994, a brutal and shadowy private army called the Ranbir Sena has carried out more than 20 massacres: fathers speared through the heart, mothers shot through the head and little children with their throats slit. The carnage on the night of February 10, 1999 was something different. Only two days earlier, the centre had despatched two companies of paramilitary forces in response to the state governments request after the Shankarbigha massacre on January 25, 1999 in which 22 Dalits were killed. The upper caste fanatics of the outlawed Ranvir Sena seemingly mocked at such official manaoeuvers by striking the sleepy Dalits hamlets in Jehamabads' Khejam Narainpur, moving down 12 Dalits in their sleep.

A private army formed in 1994 by landowners to check Naxalite influence, the Ranbir Sena is one lakh-strong. Its clashes with Dalits and the ultra left have claimed hundreds of lives. The chart below shows about the massacres of Dalits up to 1999.

In Uttar Pradesh, many people who had been classified as Sudra castes claimed a higher status. They sanskritised themselves and wanted to put on the sacred thread in order to register themselves in the census as members of the Baisya or the Kshatriya castes. This led to violent clashes between the Brahmins and Kshatriyas on the one hand and the Sudra caste on the other hand. The census report of 1921 mentioned that there was violence when the Ahirs of Northern India decided to call themselves Kshatriyas and took steps to don the sacred thread.

Date	*Place*	*District*	*Toll*
April 4,1995	Khopira	Bhojpur	3
July 25, 1995	Sarthua	Bhojpur	6
February 7, 1996	Chandi	Bhojpur	4
March 9, 1996	Patalpur	Bhojpur	3
April 12, 1996	Nonaur	Bhojpur	5
May 5, 1996	Narhi	Bhojpur	3
May 19, 1996	Narhi	Bhojpur	3
May 25, 1996	Morath	Bhojpur	3
July 11, 1996	Bathanitola	Bhojpur	22
November 26, 1996	Purhara	Bhojpur	4
December 12, 1996	Khanet	Bhojpur	5
December 24, 1996	Ekbari	Bhojpur	6
March 8, 1997	Haibaspur	Patna	10
December 1,1997	Laxmanpur-Bathe	Jehanabad	58
January 25, 1999	Shankarbigha	Jehanabad	22
February 11, 1999	Khejan Narayanur	Jehanabad	12

[*Source: India Today,* February 22, 1999, p. 22].

But S.K. Singh in his book " Pattern of Caste Tension" found that the main source of tension between the Thakurs and their traditional tenants and agricultural labourers who belong to the Ahir, Lohar and Chamar castes were land conflicts, fear of destruction of property, and mutual fear of domination by the other group. He also found that a very interesting co-relation of age with tension. The older thakurs and the younger low castes showed higher tension than the younger Thakurs and older low castes. According to this study, the older low castes were not bothered by the new situations as they had been brought upto respect the Thakurs, to accept the treatment meted out to them by the Thakurs. On the other hand, the younger persons of the low castes resented the authoritative attitude of the Thakurs. But the younger Thakurs, who have been brought up in the new society with democratic ideas, were probably looking upon the demands of the low castes as being just. Thus, there was a great tension in the minds of the older Thakurs and the younger of the low castes. The older Thakurs expected the younger people of the low castes also to behave in the same docile way in which older people were behaving.

In Maharashtra, the three dominant castes are Marathas, Brahmins and Mahars. The Brahmins have the smallest percentage of the three and yet they have, by virtue of a high level literacy and westernization among them, played a vital role in the State politics. The so called Mahars constitute the largest part of the population and play a dominant role in state politics. The congress was successful in continuously maintaining its hold over the Mahars and this factor has substantially helped it to retain power, even in 1990 elections in which Janata Dal enjoyed a strong position in other states of India particularly in neighboring Gujarat. The congress fully exploited the dominant strength of the Mahars in planning and implementing its election strategy. The Marathas constitute just 25 % of the population of the state, with largest concentrations in Kolhapur and Satara areas. They also play a leading role in Maharashtra politics. The organisation and role of Siva Sena also demonstrates a caste angle in state politics of Maharashtra.

The caste factor has also been and continues to be the most influential factor of State politics in Tamilnadu. The lower castes of Tamil Nadu became aware of their position and resented oppression and discrimination of higher castes. This change in the outlook of the lower castes led to inter-caste tensions. Broadly we can distinguish between two categories of these [a] that between Brahmins and the Non -Brahmins, and [b] that between so-called caste Hindus and Harijans.

As we have noted above, in Tamilnadu the non-Brahmin castes found themselves in a disadvantage position because the Brahmins, on account of their education, had practically a monopoly of the Government jobs. The non-Brahmin movement laid stress on two aspects—with respect to reservation in admission to the college courses and with respect to the recruitment to the government jobs. In both these they wanted that the reservation should be according to the population proportion. Both the demands created a good deal of resentment among the Brahmins who now found themselves being discriminated on the ground of their caste. However, this resentment on the part of Brahmins did not lead to any violent clashes with the non-Brahmins because elsewhere they constitute a small minority, below five per cent of the population and even more, because they cherish the ideals of tolerance and Ahimsa. Even when the members of the aggressive groups of Dravid Kazagham and Dravid Munnetra Kazagham in Tamilnadu carried on a virulent campaign against Brahmins, there were hardly any violent outburst. Generally, the Brahmins resorted to the law courts to fight against these discriminations, particularly after the adoption of the constitution which embodied the fundamental rights.

The Kallars of Ramnad district in Madras state drew up a statement prohibiting Harijans from wearing gold and silver ornaments, good clothes etc. they were also against Harijan women using flowers; they wanted to prohibit the Harijans from cooking the food in metal vessels. On the other hand, the Harijans, with a new awareness of their rights, would not put up with these demands of the caste Hindus.

In Tamilnadu, always, the Brahmins versus non-

Brahmins has been a key issue. Initially the domination of Brahmins was sought to be checked by formation of a unified non Brahmin justice Party in 1917. Its main aim was to prevent the Brahmins to get power. For this purpose, even separate electorates for the non Brahmins were demanded by the anit- Brahmin groups. The caste factor, later on, governed the organisation of the D.M.K. and it played a role in its split which led to the formation of A.I.A.D.M.K. It played a role even in respect of the once upon a time 'movement' for Dravidian separation. As Morris Jones writes, "it can be said while caste loyalty is almost everywhere present as a factor of political relations, in a state like Tamilnadu, the rapid rise of the Non- Brahmins has not merely dominated the whole safe of Tamilnadu politics, but has in particular made a significant contribution to the movement for Dravidian separatism now expressed by the Dravida Munnetra Kazgham".

When Parliament enacted the Constitution (73rd) Amendment Act in 1993 the move was hailed as a breakthrough in bringing about a vibrant system of participatory democracy at the grassroots level and a paradigm shift in the process of development. For the first time it provided for statutory reservation of elected posts in local bodies for women, besides the Scheduled Castes (Dalits) and the Scheduled Tribes. Caste Hindu leaders challenged the reservation of elected offices in local bodies for Dalits. Before the October 1996 elections, announced under he new Act, they objected in vain to the delimitation of village constituencies by the State Election Commission.

In the elections, Dalits were prevented form filing nominations in several villages where panchayat presidentships were reserved for them. Elections were held in 2002, but the elected panchayat presidents resigned within days of assuming charge under pressure from caste-Hindus.

A large number of elected Dalit and women panchayat presidents suffered humiliation at the hands of the vice presidents and co-members and even government officials. In many cases it was found that the Dalit presidents had to take orders from caste – Hindu leaders and that a substantial number of women presidents were proxies for their husbands or other men of their families. The provision in the Act that the president and the vice-president should sign cheques jointly was often used by the vice-presidents to put pressure on the presidents. In fact, in 1997, caste Hindu hostility led to the massacre of six Dalits, including Murugesan, president of the Melavalavu village panchayat in Madurai district. Caste-Hindu panchayat presidents who were sympathetic to Dalit causes were also not spared. One such panchayat chief was hacked to death in Coimbatore district.

For rural women and Dalits, most of who were elected to these posts for the first time, it was an uphill task. Fear of facting hostile people prevented them from even convening the mandatory gram sabha meetings. The police and the administrative machinery only added to their woes. The only redeeming factor was that some departments of the Central and State governments and numerous non-governmental and inter-governmental agonies, besides the Left parties and Dalit/women's organisations, tried to help them through workshops and training and capacity—building programmes, to over come the impediments. The Left parties have consistently mobilised support for them.

Six years after the three–tier panchayati raj institutions were put in place and nearly a year after the second round of elections to them were held, the ground situation with regard to the empowerment of Dalits and women appears to be changing for the better, albeit slowly. This seems to be the case at least in the southern districts of Tirunelveli and Madurai which constitute the epicenter of caste based atrocities against Dalits. While it is true that elections could not be held in five villages in this region and the elected panchayat chiefs of two villages had to lay down office, a churning process is very much visible in a number of other villages. There is a perceptible rise in the level of Dalit assertion; many Dalit and women panchayat presidents today speak with greater confidence than was the case a few years ago, and they are more aware of their rights and responsibilities.

At the other end of the spectrum, people form the dominant caste-Hindu communities and from the village orthodoxy have also indicated a change in their mindset. They possibly realise that continued hostility will not help and fear that their villages will be left out in the process of development howsoever slow it may be.

Once again the Tamil Nadu government has failed to conduct elections to fill the posts of panchayat president reserved for Dalits in four villages in the State. Defiant caste Hindu groups have been preventing these elections for nearly a decade now. While, as in the past, no nominations were received for the posts in two villages, Nattarmangalam in Madurai district and kottakkachiyendal in Virudhunagar district, the successful candidate at Keerippatti (Madurai district) V. Azhagumalai, resigned the post within minutes of assuming office on April 24, 2005.

Reservation of posts in the three-tier panchayat structure for women and the Scheduled Castes and Scheduled Tribes in one of the major features of the panchayati raj institutions that were put in place in 1996 under the Tamil Nadu Panchayats Act, 1994. Sections of caste Hindus, particularly in the southern districts, known for frequent incidents of caste-related violence, have resented reservation for Dalits from the very beginning. In the four villages, where Dalits are in a minority and depend on caste Hindu landholders for their livelihood, various methods have been adopted to stall the elections. First they prevented Dalits from filing nominations. Later, fearing the wrath of the administration, "community leaders" fielded Dalits of their choice as candidates, helped them win, and then made them resign soon after assuming charge. This has been the case in Pappapatti. The caste Hindu standpoint was that a Dalit could not be accepted as the panchayat president. "If they become presidents, we may have to show respect to them in village festivals and public functions. This we cannot do" is the common refrain.

In 2001, caste Hindus in the four villages repeated the same strategy of forcing Dalits out of the fray. In the subsequent elections held along with "casual elections", Pappapatti and Keerippatti opted to participate in the process, but only to make a mockery of it by forcing the winners not only to resign but also to plead with the state government to de-reserve their panchayats.

Eleven years have passed since the 1994 Act came into force. The Act was promulgated in the wake of the 73rd Amendment to the Constitution, which Parliament approved in 1993 with the objective of strengthening democracy at the grassroots level. The 73rd Amendment, together with the 74th, made it mandatory to establish strong, decentralised, democratically elected local bodies in rural and urban areas to achieve, the twin objectives of "economic development and social justice." A three-tier panchayati raj structure—village panchayats, panchayat unions and district panchayats and regular meetings of gram sabhas, in which all the electors are members, to involve people in the planning process are the major features of the 1994 Act. While one-third of the total number of seats have been reserved for women, Dalits' representation will be in proportion to their share in the population. The Act also ensures regular elections to the local bodies.

The performance of the Act in the past nine years has not been, by and large, disappointing. Although the functioning of the panchyatiraj institutions has been hamstrung by lack of power and finance, the political empowerment of women and Dalits has generated a lot of enthusiasm in rural Tamil Nadu. However, Dalits had to put up with countless acts of humiliation before overcoming the resistance from vested interests to a significant level.

Dalits, who account for a little over 25 per cent of the rural population in Tamil Nadu, live scattered all over the State, segregated from the rest of the people. This being the pattern of living trust upon these victims of centuries-old prejudice, they need not necessarily constitute the majority in the villages in which the posts of panchayat presidents have been reserved for Dalits. Perhaps that is why the Act has stipulated reservation for Dalits by rotation. Another apparent reason for this is the need to integrate these hitherto segregated people into mainstream society. The idea seems to that in about 40 years' time, with different panchayats being reserved for Dalits by rotation, larger sections among caste Hindus may come round to accepting the need to be more tolerant towards Dalit empowerment. Experts feel that any lenient attitude to caste Hindu resistance now would only encourage non-Dalit people in more villages to resist the inclusion of their panchayats in the list of those reserved for Dalits under the rotation system and pose a serious threat to the very system of reservation in future.

Apart from mass religious conversion a form of collective social protest experimented with by Dalits in post-Independence India is the boycott of elections, the only occasion democratic polity has given marginalised sections such as Dalits and tribal people to assert their rights and press their demands, by virtue of their sheer numbers. In the case of poll boycotts, Dalits have to face immediate resistance from not only the oppressive castes but also from the ruling political dispensation, which takes the protest as a challenge to its authority. The disapproval of this mode of protest by the state is rooted in the fact that it was first restored to by Left extremists, who do not have faith in parliamentary democracy. In the case of Dalits, tribes and other marginalised sections of people, however, decisions to boycott elections are taken locally, more in protest against the failure of the state machinery to redress their grievances than on any ideological grounds. This form of protest by Dalits is apparently in a nascent stage and is yet to prove its efficacy. When the people of Gundupatti in Dindigul district tried this in the 1998 parliamentary elections, the administration and the ruling party did not take kindly to it and reacted ruthlessly.

A recent example comes from Kalapatti village on the outskirts of Coimbatore. During the run-up to the parliamentary elections, the Dalits of the village announced their decision to boycott the elections on the ground that many of their grievances remained unaddressed. One of their principal demands was that they be allowed entry into the common village temple. The predominant caste-Hindus in the village have been resisting their demand for many years now. Neither the State government nor the Sangh Parivar, which wielded considerable influence among Dalits of the region, could do anything about it. The Dalits, however, were firm on their decision. It is said that when the president of the State unit of the Bharatiya Janata Party (BJP) visited the village for campaigning, Dalits were indifferent to his visit, which infuriated BJP workers. The local caste-Hindus also were critical of the Dalits' boycott decision.

On May 16, 2004 a mob of 200 persons belonging to the predominant caste Hindu community of Grounders, all armed with weapons, allegedly entered Shastri Nagar and New Colony, both Dalit settlements of Kalpatti village and ransacked about 100 Dalit houses, causing damage to television sets and other household items. They burnt down about 20 houses and damaged another 12. When the residents attempted to run for safety, they were assaulted with weapons such as long sticks, iron rods, knives and sickles.

The attack at Kalapatti is significant in more than one respect. It is the first time that caste-related violence of such magnitude has been reported in the western region of Tamil Nadu. The Arun Thathiyar, who form the predominant Dalit group in the region, are the most neglected Dalits in the State. Mostly cobblers and scavengers, they seem to be the poorest of the community, and have been victims of the worst forms of untouchability for centuries. Unlike the Pallars in southern Tamil Nadu and the Parayars of the northern region, a substantial number of whom have had some access to education and are increasingly becoming aware of their rights and privileges, the Aruthathiyars remain backward, socially, politically and economically. Only in recent times have they been organised under Dalit organisation.

Ironically, until recently, Hindutva forces were using Arunthathiyar youth for violent activities in and around Coimbatore. Dalit leaders say that the Kalapatti incident only shows that the Sangh Parivar, which is apparently losing its hold over the Arunthathiyars as is evidenced by the latter's decision to boycott the election in which the BJP was trying to retain its seat, and the predominant caste-Hindus are intolerant of these voiceless people achieving political awareness and organising themselves.

Caste prejudices are deep-rooted in Tamil Nadu, and people would even kill to preserve 'family (or caste) honour'. It is a situation where a woman is not meant to have any views of her own, not even about the man who would be her husband, all in the name of 'family honour'. Women's rights experts believe that this is based on the anachronistic but still prevalent belief among many communities, cutting across race, religion or caste, that women are the property of the men in the family and as such, do not have any right of their own to decide their future.

Dalit women, in addition to the gender bias, bear the burdens of caste and class. Studies have revealed that Dalit girls have been forced to become concubines of caste-Hindus patrons and village priests at several places. Dalit women are routinely subjected to sexual abuse and related offences by caste-Hindu landlords and their family members, these studies show. In fact, at Siruthondamadevi, for the last 10 years Dalit families have been sending their grownup daughters to welfare centres in Chennai and Pondicherry, to save them from such sexual harassment. "Life for women here is like coexisting with fire," said Palaniammal, 34 of the village, which has 100 Dalit families and 1,500 Vanniya families. Barring a few, all the Dalit families are Christians and most of them work as labourers in the Vanniyas' farms.

Dalit-Vanniya tensions in the village came to a head on April 14, B.R. Ambedkar's birth anniversary. Caste-Hindus objected to the celebrations organised by Dalits and to the hoisting of a party flag on the grounds that no political party can hoists its flag in the village under a "(informal) panchayat" decision. Dalit youth said that using this as a pretext, Vanniyas entered the Dalit "colony" and went on the rampage. They assaulted men and women, ransacked homes and damaged their belongings.

Dalits of the village subjected to several forms of "untouchability". They were not allowed to use footwear while crossing places where caste-Hindu people lived and that they were not allowed to ride two-wheelers when caste-Hindus were around. They could not drive their bullock carts through "upper caste" streets, and whenever they saw a caste-Hindu person they had to get down and push the cart. Their children did not have access to the only primary school in the village, run by the panchayat union. No Dalit children has been admitted in the school for more than two decades now. They went to schools in the neighboring village.

Dalit women were asked to wait for long hours at the Public Distribution System outlet located in the caste-Hindu area, and often they did not get their supplies. They and their men were forced to work long hours in the Vanniya landholders' fields and households for meager payments. Agricultural workers, had to pay a fine if they absented themselves from work. Not even the relatively well-off Dalits were spared.

A fact-finding team of the All India Democratic Women's Association (AIDWA), which visited the village, demanded the government's intervention to initiate inquiries into the charges made by Dalit women and to take prompt action for providing relief to the affected Dalits. Unless the government had the political will to eradicate "untouchability" and took serious efforts in that direction, discrimination against and harassment of these marginalised people could not be stopped.

Caste and conversion politics in Tamilnadu always deserves a national concern. Ever since Dr. B.R. Ambedkar embraced Buddhism along with about five lakh Dalits in 1956, mass conversion has become a form of collective protest for Dalits across the country, a willing abandonment of what they consider an oppressive hierarchical social system. The rejection of a system as a form of protest gets reinforced by necessarily choosing one of the available alternative systems. In a society where religious sentiments are deep-rooted, leaving one's religion can be a hard choice. Conversions, therefore, take place at a slow pace. It is for this reason that a legal ban on conversions is often considered unwarranted.

In Tamil Nadu, the conversion of about 200 Dalit families to Islam at Meenakshipuram in Tirunelveli district in the early 1980s drew nationwide attention. Although all sorts of ulterior motives were attributed to their conversion, the converts remain loyal Muslims and claim that they now live with "greater social respect" than before, which they were yearning for. Yet no mass conversion has taken place since then.

Hindutva forces, however, have often raised the bogey of attempts by Muslim and Christians to convert Hindus on a large scale through pressure, force or allurement and demanded a ban on conversions. Denying that there was any "force" or "allurement" from anybody, the Dalits say that though they have had a predominant presence in the village and their panchayat has had a Dalit head for many years, they are not treated by caste-Hindus as equals in any respect. They feel they don not enjoy social respect and this has been an affront to their self-respect.

Although many Dalits in the village, including family members of those who have already opted to convert, have reservations about leaving the Hindu fold, they confirm that the caste-Hindus, even small boys, disrespectfully call Dalit elders by their names. "More than anything else, the verbal abuse hurts to them.

In fact, they convert knowing full well that they will lose the benefits of reservation and concessions they at present enjoy. In his view, Dalits who convert are on the whole not economically dependent on caste-Hindus for survival; they have been victims of social oppression of one form or the other. Dalits who shun a confrontationist course for various reasons also go in for conversion.

Caste has deep roots in Karnataka politics. The main contending castes have been the Lingayats and Okkalingas. The Lingayats have managed to dominate the political scene most of the time. From 1947 to 1957, the Okkalingas dominated the political scene but after that Lingayats have been dominating the political scene in Karnataka.

The power struggle in Kerala reflects a struggle between the Nayars and Ezahavas. The communist parties of Kerala have used caste factor to their advantage in getting the power to govern this small state of Indian union which has the distinction of being the most educated state. Prof. Harrison has rightly observed, "the success of the Kerela Communist Party as the first regional communist party in India to capture control of a state Government can be explained, above all, to the ability to manipulate politically strategic caste lobbies. The Kerela communists were able to transform economic despair into a legislative majority because of their footing on regional caste ground, notably among the numerous Ezahavas provided the necessary margin of Block strength in the necessary constituencies". However, it must be pointed out that in Kerela the caste factor has played a secondary role because religion has been the primary factor in state politics.

Like in other parts of India, the renaissance movement in Kerala was entirely indigenous. This revolt in Kerala was against the caste-ridden feudal society with its hierarchical system which wiped out all individuality and suppressed everyone, but the highest under the iron heels of customs and traditions. There were scores of castes and subcastes in society, everyone of which considered itself superior to the one just below it and oppressed the latter, the former being in turn subjected to the same oppression by the caste immediately above. At the top were the Nambudiri Brahmins who were also the owners of the entire land in Kerala. This double supremacy of caste and landed wealth reinforced by the sacred injections of Sastras and Smritis kept the lower castes in subjugation. The status of the lower castes like Pulayas and Parayas was nothing better than that of the slaves even after their formal emancipation towards the later part of the nineteenth century by the royal edict.

There were also strict rules with regard to

untouchability. The Pulaya could not come within a certain distance of Ezhava, the Ezhava had to keep a certain distance from the Nair, the Nair could not touch a Nambudiri and so on and so forth. There was even the peculiar custom of the Paraya or Nayadi — the lowest of the castes in Kerala — making loud noises while walking along public roads so that if any high caste person was approaching he could know and then the lower caste man had to run away from the road and keep himself at a safe distance.

No reform of such a society was possible without a down right attack upon the whole hierarchical system of caste and the assertion of human dignity. This necessary task was undertaken by a whole galaxy of reformers, the first and foremost among whom was Shree Narayan Guru. The movement of Narayan Guru for the abolition of untouchability was a truly national movement in Kerala and it churned up the entire people during the early decades of the twentieth century.

Haryana is no exception to the general observation that caste factor dominates state politics in India. Jats-Ahirs, and Brahmins, Constitute the two active caste groups of Haryana. A Jat votes for Jat and an Ahir votes for Ahir is an accepted principle and it guides the selection of candidates for various constitutencies, the election campaign and the voting pattern. The Jats have tended to dominate Haryana politics and they are anti-Congress. The leadership of Choudhary Devi Lal rested upon Jat support and his leadership pattern clearly reflected typical Jat culture. This was true of Om Prakash Chautala's government. Congress in Haryana mostly depends upon the support of Brahmins and Ahirs. The organisation of Gujjar Sammelans and Brahmin Sammelans in Haryana fully demonstrates the big role of caste in state politics. Caste based electoral violence is a sad fact of Haryana politics.

Devi Lal of Haryana, had organized caste combination

of Ahirs, Jats, Gujjars and Rajputs (AJGAR) to unleash the political 'python' on its rivals. This strategy of caste politics may help achieve some immediate political and economic gains, but it is not likely to pay the states concerned and the country in the long run.

Gujarat saw the formation of a powerful and influential caste federation in the Kshatriya Sabha in 1948. It represented many castes and lineage groups, most of them drawn from the economically depressed communities of cultivators. For about two decades, it acted as a powerful pressure group in the politics of that state. In the early seventies, Madhav Singh Solanki formed a coalition of Kshatriyas, Harijans, Adivasis and Muslims known as 'KHAM' to cut the dominant Patels of the state down to size. Much of the turmoil that Gujarat state witnessed during the seventies and the early eighties can be, in a manner of speaking, traced to the cynical resort to such brazen caste politics.

In Rajasthan also, the caste factor has been an active factor of state politics.

The strong differences between the Jats and Rajputs have in the past enabled Brahmins to control power. The chief ministers of Rajasthan have been mostly Brahmins. The Rajput's support for BJP was a major factor behind its success in the 1996 elections. However, caste and religion together and not individually act as the determinants of politics in Rajasthan.

Within Hinduism, the Dalits continue to battle for dignity. From outside, they are offered equality before the eyes of a different God and His disciples. Some still hope for the former. Some have given up all hope. Like Harishanker Bairwa, a Dalit and former member of the Vishwa Hindu Parishad who was a kar sevak during the Babri Masjid demolition. Harishankar recently called upon his community to "give up this religion, which thinks we are less than human".

In Rajasthan, a community of Dalits was persecuted by upper caste Jats for using a temple tank. The Supreme Court judgement that non-Brahmins, including Dalits, can become temple priests may have gladdened some Dalit hearts, but not this particular community. One can only wonder what they thought of the ordinance issued by the Tamil Nadu Government banning conversions by the use of force or allurements.

By taking a dip in a tank to use of which was restricted to the Jats and Meenas of the Chakwara village, Babulal Bairwa, a former security guard, unwittingly set off a Chain reaction that led to the Dalits deciding to convert to Buddhism. Strangely, it was not the Rajputs who objected to Babulal's use of the pond but the Jats, who, a couple of years ago got themselves declared as backward class in order to become eligible for reservation in government jobs. Babulal's dip in the pond led to the entire Bairwa community being fined Rs. 50,000 by the Jat dominated village panchayat. When they refused to pay, the community was excommunicated. "No one would sell us anything, give us work or talk to us".

On September 21, 2002 a Sadbavana march by the Bairwas to the village pond was blocked by nearly 20,000 Jats and Meenas gathered from the nearby villages. Violence erupted with nearly 10 policemen being injured. As of now, the Dalits are bathing in the pond under police protection, while the Jats and Meenas have stopped using it.

Dalits everywhere, who have at one time or the others suffered humiliation and worse from the upper castes, are echoing that sentiment. They are also working to gain the political clout necessary to ensure that the existing laws on untouchability and other discriminatory practices are enforced. To the extent that it is any consolation, the courts have often ruled in their favour. As Eleanor Zelliott, professor emeritus at Carleton College, Minnesota, and the author of *'From Untouchables to Dalit: Essays on the Ambedkar Movement'* wrote, "Unlike in the past where laws and legislation followed social reform movements, today we see an increasing trend of activists using progressive laws as levers to affect reform".

The latest being the Supreme Court verdict that effectively breaks the monopoly of the Brahmins' control of temples—an important source of wealth, patronage and influence throughout the country. "This verdict is like a beam of light at the end of a tunnel." Says Bojja Tarrakkam, a senior Andhra Prades-high Court advocate. "Dalits had begun to shun the temples as they had become a symbol of upper caste supremacy." Said Avantika Prasad Marmath, president of Ujjain's Dalit Sahitya Academy. "This decision will restore our faith in temples."

The courts will probably soon have to take up another contentious issue, the Tamil Nadu ordinance promulgated by governor P.S. Ramamohan Rao just a fortnight ahead of the scheduled Assembly session, banning conversions by force or allurements, with stringent punishments for those found guilty. And where it is by choice, the law insists the district magistrate be informed within a specified period. Christian organisations were quick to criticise the ordinance.

Many Dalit intellectuals view the ordinance as anti-constitutional. "It works against the Dalits," said M. Lakshmaiah, coordinator, Centre for Dalit Studies in Hyderabad. "In Tamil Nadu the current rulers are the upper Shudra communities such as the Vanniyars, Chettiars, Nadars, etc. They fought against Brahminism and attacks against Dalits, at one time. These people have now become

Brahmins themselves, which means they are against the Dalits."

Predictably, outfits like the Hindu Munnani and Sangh parivar members like the VHP, who have for long been demanding state intervention to stop conversions, have welcomed it. Kanchi Sankaracharya Sri Jayendra Saraswati said the law would be a check against communal tensions, and other states should follow suit.

This support, of course, does not address the core issues of untouchability offences and the many instances of oppression of Dalits by upper caste Hindus, as documented in a study by the National Commission for Scheduled Caste /Scheduled Tribe.

Roadside, dhabas in Punjab do not have separate tea-cups for Dalits, and Dalits are not massacred when they ask for higher wages: and that, it is now becoming clear, is about as far equality goes in India's most prosperous State.

On June 5, 2003 Dalits and the dominant landholding Jat community blew apart the façade of caste peace in Punjab, initiating clashes that left one person dead and dozens injured. The clashes began at an annual fair held at the Shaheed Baba Nihal Sing Samadhi, built in memory of a local Sufi saint in Talhan village near Jalandhar. Most of the injured were Dalits and most of the 10 homes damaged in the rioting also belonged to Dalits. A 27 year-old Dalit, Vijay Kumar Kala, was killed in police firing, which began after Dalits torched buses and blocked traffic on the Jalandhar-Amritsar railway line.

Violent clashes between the police and Dalits continued in Jalandhar for several days. Although curfew was imposed in Talhan, fresh clashes broke out there on June 8, 2003. This time, Dalit assertion was evident.

The violence in Jalandhar mirrored this local conflagration, with young Dalits refusing to respect curfew orders imposed by what they said is a Jat-dominated police force and administration. The violence had, without dispute, been the worst caste-related strife Punjab has ever seen.

It all began a decade ago, when massive donations by overseas Punjabis began to flow into the coffers of the until-then obscure Shaheed Baba Nihal Singh Shrine. The Dalits soon began to assert that they had a right to share in the management of the shrine, since it was built on village common land. The matter went to court and last January Dalits obtained an order enabling them to participate in elections to the shrine's managing committee. Jats flatly refused to respect the order, and the matter went back to court. On January 14 this year, Dalits, armed with a fresh court order, arrived again to contest the elections. This time Jats walked out.

Talhan's Dalits chose to assert their rights. Since Jats had walked out of the elections, all 13 members of the committee chosen that day were Dalits. The same day Jats announced an economic blockade of Dalits, by refusing to buy their milk, sell them fodder, and even denying them access to open fields to defecate.

Talhan's Jats have found support both in the mainstream SGPC, which has blamed the violence there on the Bharatiya Janata Party, and far-Right organisations such as the Damadami Taksal. Talhan, in a very direct way, poses a challenge to Jat hegemony over Sikh religious practices, with sects like the Ad-Dharmis asserting their right to control community institutions. Equally, the incident posed a serious challenge to secular forces in Punjab.

While religion as a factor in electoral politics broke through the surface of efforts to make the choice of Indian voters rational, caste remained an important determinant of voting behaviour during the last general elections of 1989 and 1991. Students of Indian politics have known it for decades that Congress's power in the villages had arisen from its successful mobilization of two separate categories of castes, each of which proved aggregatable into rudimentary class formations at election time. These were the landless Harijans at the bottom of rural society and the elite castes at the top.

Not only congress but opposition parties too have structured their political power on caste categories. The basis upon which certain opposition parties survived even landslide victories for the congress, as in 1984, was crucial. Lok Dal, which was the most viable opposition to Congress in most of the Hindi belt was originally perceived as another in the long line of caste movements that left their mark on modern Indian history. It appealed primarily to those castes in the rural areas who as cultivators and herders were preached along the border the ritually unclean castes. This middle class peasant mobilization by the opposition could be viewed as a sociological reflex of Congress's own caste strategy in the rural sector.

One of the main features of the last two Lok Sabha elections was an uncertain electoral verdict. Some observers have been tempted into the comforting thought that the present Lok Sabha, as the one before it, represents an electoral aberration and that its composition is fortuitous. Such a notion appears to be mistaken. The changes in the composition of central and state legislatures and particularly in Uttar Pradesh and Bihar, show that they reflect the changing balance of power in caste terms. Such changes have been visible in the political mobilization of middle caste communities from 1967 onwards. It commenced as Samyukta Vidhayak Dal around 1968, evolved through a series of permulations (BKD, LD) between 1960 and the mid 1970's joined Janata to defeat Congress in 1977 and was a constituent of the Janata Dal that managed to get the second largest number of seats in 1989. This was the middle caste peasants answer to congress's alleged predilection towards those segments of rural society (The elite caste and the Harijans) which posed obstacles to his own aspirations. The earlier disproportionately large representation of the upper castes in the state legislatures came down during the last two elections while the number of middle caste legislators has gone up considerably. This social and political development is now visible at the national level too.

The emergence of Janata Dal as the second largest party in Lok Sabha in 1989 and its decision to implement the Mandal Commission Report tied one more knot in India's contorted caste-based politics. Janata Dal's campaign for social justice and equality was aimed at carving a permanent constituency for itself among the upwardly mobile middle castes, which had been termed as OBC's or other backward classes by the Mandal Commission to distinguish them from Scheduled Castes and Tribes which find mention in the constitution of India. This strategy helped the Janata Dal to almost completely sweep the Lok Sabha Polls in Bihar and perform reasonably well in Uttar Pradesh in 1991. The Mandal card played a vital role in Bihar in consolidating the backward class segments votes, which constitute 70 per cent of the population in almost all the constituencies of the state, in favour of the Janata Dal.

The impact of the backward classes movement in North India in recent years, particularly in Bihar and Uttar Pradesh, has to be seen against the background of political mobilization of caste in other parts of India. The emergence of party configurations out of dispersed and fragmented caste identities has taken a large diversity of forms. In Tamilnadu, building upon the early anti-Brahmin movement there took place a wide spectrum of lower caste assertions, getting consolidated in Dravida and Tamil identities. In Andhra Pradesh and Karnataka the political ascendancy of middle peasant castes was followed by responses from castes still lower down. In Kerala caste identities became rallying points for party formations, starting with the

Ezhawas, at one time the most backward of all communities. Given the highly plural and regionally federal structure of social and cultural reality in India, politicization of caste has not produced one single formation. Yet, in almost all the states, and of late even at the center, the role of caste has been an important factor in determining electoral fortunes. Caste, like religion, has served to make democratic politics intelligible to the masses in India.

The BJP in Maharashtra was known as the party of Brahmans and the merchants. However the election of 1989 demonstrated that the BJP-Siva sena alliance had made strong inroads in the Congress castle in Maharashtra state-Brahmins, Marathas, OBCs and the Scheduled castes preferred the BJP- Siva Sena alliance to the Congress. Except the Scheduled castes among the Hindus, more Hindus preferred BJP-Siva Sena alliance. The Bharatiya Republican Party (BRP) could secure some votes of OBCs, SCs and Neo-Buddhists. However, what was significant was that the rest of them voted for Congress and alliance. Janata Dal faired very badly, but it had votes in all the castes. It has been pointed out that although castes and political parties extend support and make use of each other for their ends, yet such, an alliance cannot be final or permanent. This is so because a political party cannot devote itself entirely on caste interest, as it has various other interests to look after and also runs by certain ideology, thus cutting across simple caste prejudices. In India there is hardly any instance of a political party being identified really with a particular caste group.

For a region that has a history of social revolution, the alliance between the Shiv Sena and the faction of the Republican Party of India (RPI) led by Ramdas Athavale is some thing of a setback. Such an alliance will work to the advantage of the Sena, but for Dalits the scales are tilted more towards losses than gains. There was nothing momentous about the occasion when Athavale and the

Shiv Sena's newly appointed leader Uddhav Thackeray, met in mid-February 2003. It has to be understood that the offer was made keeping in mind the realities of State politics. Sushil Kumar Shinde was made the Chief Minister because of his merit, he was a Dalit. In the all-India context, choosing a Dalit to lead Maharashtra at this particular political juncture is a relevant and important factor. With this open offer, the Sena sending a message of support to Bhim Shakti [Ambedkarites], telling it that if they work together they can make Maharashtra prosperous."

However, two facts can not be ignored. One, if the RPI (Athavale) accepts the Sena's offer it will destabilise the Dalit movement. Two, the RPI leadership has failed to gauge the feelings of the Dalit community at large.

Dalit perceptions of the Sena are primarily negative. The Sena had played a major part in the violence in 1994 after the renaming of Marathwada University as Dr. Babasaheb Ambedkar University. The sena blew out of proportion certain remarks made by Dr. Ambedkar in his work 'Riddles of Hinduism' and demanded a ban on its publication. The Sena has rejected the ideal of reservation for Dalits in education or in jobs. During the riots in the BDD chawls in Mumbai in 1974, Sainiks clashed with RPI activists. And it was during Sena- Bharatiya Janata Party rule in Maharashtra that 11 Dalits were killed in police firing in Ramabai Nagar, in Mumbai. The Left parties and the Peasants and Workers Party (PWP) are the natural political allies of Dalits. Other Backward Classes (OBCs) who constitute the majority of Sena supporters and workers, are closer to Dalits than the Marathas, that the RPI is a puppet of the Congress (I) and the NCP. "There may be only one Dalit family in the village, but it will fly the flag of Dr. Babasaheb Ambedkar. Dalits are present everywhere. The only problem is that they are divided. If they stand united, the RPI can even rule the Brihan Mumbai Municipal Corporation. In Mumbai the power of Dalits is great because of rural migration. Of the documented 40 per cent of migrants who enter the city, 95 per cent are Dalits. Yet, they have not won even a single ward in Mumbai, because of factionalism."

When there is an incident, for instance a police firing, in a Dalit slum, the entire community comes together. "The people are together for the cause but the leaders are fractious."

Isolated working examples of Sena RPI alliance already exist in some local bodies in the State. However, at the moment the Shiv Sena has cleverly left the offer open. It is not insisting that the RPI accept Hindutva; it is seeking a political alliance. It can afford to wait since it will be the ultimate beneficiary.

The point is that Dalits already have the law on their side. They have the numbers. Social reforms have already been initiated. There is no indication that an alliance with the Sena will be any better than an alliance with the Congress (I) or the National Congress Party (NCP). What is required is a united RPI, but that tragically, is something the party's own leaders are opposed to.

However, we do come across certain castes lending strong support to particular political parties. Political parties and caste groups are thus interdependent on each other and one can not survive without the support of other. Thus, while political parties struggle among themselves to win different caste groups in their favour by making offers to them, caste groups try to pressurize parties to choose its members for candidature in elections. If the caste group is dominant and political party is an important one, this interaction is all the more prominent.

As far as Bihar is concerned "Every election witnesses the emergence of renewed caste bitterness. Even the political parties, in place of ideological polarization, there occur the determination of policies and programmes as well as the nomination of electoral candidates and the extension of support to gain on caste consideration. Bihar, has been severely plague with caste problems because the notorious vestiges of a decedent feudalism have been quite prevalent here. Due to inadequate and limited economic and educational opportunities, kinship considerations have always been prominent here. Because of the feudal vestiges and caste consciousness in Bihar, there is almost always a clash between ideological and social considerations in the voting pattern. Infact political parties, and members of government and administration feel impact of caste.

It can be seen that the upper caste have always been in a more or less dominant position in spite of being a numerical minority, this group and minorities generally supported the congress, where as the backward castes have generally turned towards the other opposition parties. In the pre 1967 era the tussle for power in congress remained confined within the upper caste groups. With the slow emergence of the backwards, the party has tried to extend its representation to all sections of the people, but it is the upper castes which continue to holds sway over the party. Infact, previously the same was the case with other opposition parties too, excluding the SSP (samajuakta socialist party) which sought support among the lower middle and the lower castes. The Jharkhand, a regional party has always sought support among the tribals. The 1967 and 1977 elections saw the congress parties defeat and found the backwards emerge as a strong force in the political arena. One of the most important reasons which resulted in the unprecedented defeat of the congress party in the state in 1967 election was the exploitation of the sentiments of backward castes again the continued domination of the upper castes in the congress party, by the opposition parties, especially by the Samyukta socialist party, which had formed a united front consisting of most of the opposition parties before the elections and made anti-congressism, its main slogan in the polls. The elections how ever, did best lead to a social polarization between the backwards and the forwards, it also helped the backwards to make their presence felt in the political fields. The opposition parties had no doubt helped in developing this process. The backward-forward division became more sharp after the 1977 election when Karpoor Thakur took over the reins of administration.

The 1977 elections, had special significance as all non–Leftist opposition parties united under the banner of the Janata Party and fought the elections against the Congress. In this election the upper caste was in majority in all parties except the last category comprising independents and other groups. The backward castes were next to the upper caste in almost all parties and they occupied the maximum number of seats in the independents and other groups. The percentage of upper caste members was highest in the CPM i.e., fifty per cent although obtaining only two seats. The Janta, Congress and Independent category found response from all castes and communities. The backward castes group secured the next position in all parties except independent group where this group secured the highest percentage. Interestingly this group secured the same number of seats (21) as the upper caste in the Congress, which was a rare event. It appears that during the political upheaval of the Janata party, the backward caste group did not betray the Congress. The contribution of scheduled castes in Janata Party was significant (39 candidates) and was insignificant (2 candidates) in the Congress. They also contributed four seats and two seats to the C.P.I and independent groups respectively. Scheduled tribes contributed significantly to the Janata Party, securing 18 seats. The C.P.I. and C.P.M. secured one seat each, whereas independent group received four seats. The contribution of Muslims and Bengalies was nil in C.P.I. and C.P.M. The maximum number of Muslim seats was secured by Janata party (14 seats), followed by Congress (8 seats) and independent groups (3 seats).

In tne 1980 elections, the upper caste was in majority in the Congress (I), Janata (J.P.), B.J.P., C.P.M. and among independent and others. Jharkhanda Mukti Morcha did not have any upper caste member; it being a representative of mainly tribal interests. In Lok Dal and C.P.I the backwards prevailed over the upper castes. The response of this group towards the C.P.M was nil. The Scheduled castes secured the second position in the C.P.I, but the C.P.M could not return any member either from the scheduled castes and scheduled tribes. Even among the Congress (U), Lok Dal and Janata Party the contribution of scheduled tribes was nil. The scheduled tribes secured the highest percentage in the Jharkhand Mukti Morcha and after that the B.J.P.

The caste position in the legislative assembly after the elections of 1985 was that, the upper castes secured the highest percentage in Janta Party. Jharkhand Mukti Morcha secured scheduled tribe majority. The C.P.M. secured one seat in the Assembly which went to the Bengali. The scheduled castes secured the highest percentage in the Lok Dal. The Congress (I) was the only party which returned members from all castes and communities.

In the 1989 elections the Congress remained the only party which did not enter into any alliance with any political party, regional or national and decided to contest all the 54 seats in the State. The ploy of having a Rajput chief minister to neutralize the influence of V.P. Singh and also Chandra Sekhar did not pay any dividend and the party emerged highly bruised and humiliated out of the electoral battle. Even the Congress this time made serious endeavours to induct as many backward community candidates as possible. But the gimmick did not work. The Janta Dal, on the other hand, stole a march over others by inducting as many as 14 OBC candidates. The distribution of tickets different political parties once again proved that Yadvas, Kurmis, Koers and Banias enjoy considerable political influence in the State, and they cornerd most of the seats. The Janta Dal nominated 14 OBCs, CPI 7 and the B.J.P. 8. Among the nominees the Yadavas raced far ahead of others. If in the Janta Dal, 9 were Yadavas, 7 were the C.P.I nominees. Three Yadavs found mention in the B.J.P. list. However the Congress remained the only party to allow representation to Banias. In addition, most of the candidates, set up by Lok Dal (B) and IPF came from OBCs. It bears testimony to the growing influence of OBCs in the Bihar Politics.

In Bihar all the parties play the caste card to the best of the capacity in every election. Even top most leaders like Laloo Prasad Yadav did not care for giving blatant casteist speeches. The following vignette cites a glaring example: "Oh ! you mothers and sisters with knots in your hair. Do you know why for generations you have had these untidy knotted hairs? because the Purohit (the Brahim priest), has told you that knotted hair was a boon of Lord Siva. (Lord Siva is known for Jataen or knotted hair). This is a lie. The purohit wants you to believe that your knotted hair is Siva's boon because he does not want you to have access to soap, shampoo and a comb. After all, if knotted hair was a boon of Shiva why does Jagannath Mishra's wife not have knotted hair?"

Here, it can be noted that Congress leader, Jagannath Mishra, is a Maithili Brahmin, on the higher rungs of the caste hierarchy. Of course, class difference regularized and institulised as in caste structure. The Hindu Muslim equation was obvious and was always discussed. When this equation degenerated into communalism, the discussion continued, some times mindlessly. But the Bramhnical system had imposed a taboo on any public discussion on caste. Any discussion on a rigid structure, which has endured centuries, would have been tantamount to subverting it.

While discussion was discouraged, the whole structure was exposed to western notions of egalitarianism, equity, social justice, upward mobility. The result is that this ancient and secure structure is now wobbly and in the process of rapid change. These changes are hitting us in the face through the unseemly process of electoral populism.

Who would be the Prime Minister of India after the 1996 general election? In the event of a coalition at the centre, which of the two formations would be the Congress be more comfortable with? This was a sensitive question for Congress man those days because an individual congress man's gravitation towards the BJP or the Laloo Yadav type "National Front" formations was likely to be determined primarily by the caste factor. For example, a losing, upper caste congress man was more inclined to shift towards the BJP, not because he had suddenly been attracted by saffron, but because he was likely to find greater caste affinity among the BJP. By the same token a lower caste congress man in decline would be more comfortable with Laloo Prasad Yadav, with Murali Manohar Joshi or Atal Bihari Bajapaye. Since 1996 marked the end of congress dominance at the centre, the question of coalition partners the party was likely to choose was of singular importance.

The large middle class everyone talks about, the one which influences opinion at nodal points, was likely divided on that issue. The English speaking managerial-cum-bureaucratic class was likely to throw its weight behind a congress-B.J.P coalition at the centre, largely because for him caste and class had become conterminous. The more homespun middle class was comfortable with regional formations like Deve Gowda's or N.T. Rama Rao's. The new middle class which had sprung up from the ranks of the lower castes over the last few decades quite naturally, supported backward caste leaders like Laloo Prasad Yadav and Mulayum Singh Yadav. In Uttar Pradesh and Bihar the coming together of the congress and BJP support bases was largely a manifestation of caste consolidation. That was the consequence of a forward backward polarization and sheer numbers tilted the scales in favour of the backward castes. When V.P. Singh raised the Mandal Commission report to mobilize the backwards, the BJP retaliated by accelerating the Ram Janma Bhumi agitation. In other words, the Mandir movement sought to sharpen the Hindu Muslim divide with the desired objectives of Hindu consolidation to arrest caste polarization in spite the Mandal. But for the 199 UP Assembly election, the BJP high command alerted by the caste factor, gave tickets to a large number of backward caste candidates and ultimately elected a lower caste Lodh Kalyana Singh as Chief Minister.

Another significant development which the 1989 elections highlighted was the emergence of Bahujan Samaj Party (B.S.P) as the spokesman of the scheduled castes and the depressed sections. The party which emerged as a social organization in 1980, contested election for the first time in March 1985 for the U.P State Assembly and to the Lok Sabha in Allahabad in 1988 securing third position. Though it secured 3 out of the total 105 seats it contested, it stood up to be seen scence and counted. In 73 Lok Sabha and 260 assembly constituencies it secured second and third position. It seems that the B.S.P has plundered traditional scheduled castes votes from the congress and its impact was visible in the most of the constituencies of Vindhya and Chatisgarh region of Northern Madhya Pradesh. At present, however, it was responsible for draining away much of the scheduled castes votes from the all the major political parties and particularly congress.

The caste-oriented politics of Uttar Pradesh entered a new era on June 9,2005 with the Brahmin Maha Rally organised by the Bahujan Samaj Party (BSP) in Lucknow.

Almost every feature of the rally, from its noticeable social and political facets to its not-so-distinct dimensions of realpolitik, denoted that politics in the State was acquiring new qualitative and quantitative characteristics. It indicated that the cauldron of caste politics in Uttar Pradesh would witness some new churning in the days to come.

To start with, it was for the first time in the history of the State that a party professing essentially to champion the interests of "the oppressed Dalit community" organised a rally dedicated exclusively to the interests of the community at "the highest end" of the very caste system that the party used to term "oppressive". Second, and perhaps more interestingly, the response, in terms of numbers, from the Brahmin community to the call from the "Dalit party" was not insignificant. Third, the call and the response to it provoked discussions about the development of a new and powerful social combination- comprising Dalits, Brahmins and Muslims – capable of significantly impacting electoral equations in Uttar Pradesh.

The most conspicuous element of the rally was the BSP's change of attitude towards Brahmins and vice versa. Almost all the happenings at the rally, from the manner in which BSP president and former Chief Minister Mayawati was greeted and received at the venue to the speeches made by the leaders and the response from the participants, highlighted this change.

As Mayawati arrived at the venue, she was greeted with Brahminical rituals. A group of priests chanted Vedic hymns and blew conches. Responding to the reception, Mayawati said that her party was never against the upper castes or the Hindu religion. "We were branded as anti-upper castes and anti-Hindu by Manuvadi vested interests, including, political parties and sections of the media." In stating this, Mayawati gave up the one slogan – "Tilak, tarazu aur talwar inko maro joote chaar" (thrash the

Brahmin, the Bania and the Rajput with shoes) – that helped the BSP to aggressively pursue its pro-Dalit agenda during the 1980s and 1990s. The BSP chief's contention was that none of her party leaders had ever raised the slogan. She added that the BSP was only opposed to certain discriminatory tendencies and attitudes prevalent in Hindu society, such as caste oppression, and not to the upper castes as such.

In a clear political message, she added that the new, growing positive appreciation of the BSP among the State's Brahmins would be beneficial for the community in electoral terms because the party leadership had decided to give the ticket to more members of the community in all future elections.

But not everybody is ready to accept this theorisation that seeks to highlight the BSP's overtures to Brahmins in terms of the party's philanthropic ideals. According to Ramakanth Vajpayee, a former BJP activist who is currently associated with the BSP initiative, the present process is a marriage of convenience for both the party and sections of the Brahmin community in the State. He pointed out: "The BSP, like all other big parties in the State, has realised that it has reached a saturation point of support within its core caste support base in the Dalit Chamar Community. Its leadership knows that it has to win over other communities if it has to enhance its strength and influence in the State's polity, and hence the new love for Brahmins."

It was the BJP that first tried to add value to its core support base by bringing together social groups beyond that base. This was done right from the early 1990s by projecting the concept of a pan-Hindu identity. The party clubbed its manifestly upper-caste Hindutva ideology with the projection of Other Backward Class (OBC) leaders such as Kalyan Singh, Uma Bharati and Vinay Katiyar,

S.P. leader and Chief Minister Mulayam Singh Yadav and party general secretary Amar Singh followed the same strategy in a different form when they successfully forged a social combination of the OBC Yadav community with Muslims and Thakurs during the past decade. In short, all the parties devised ways and means to add a new community to their core caste-based vote banks. The outcomes of the last few elections in the State have underscored this trend. The BSP's Brahmin initiative clearly belongs to this genre.

But what motivated Mayawati and the BSP to woo the Brahmin community? One of the factors, according to BSP ideologues, is that there is greater social compatibility between Dalits and Brahmins than there is between Dalits and intermediate castes such as Yadavs. Kanshi Ram, the BSP founder, told in 1995 that the alliance with upper castes, especially Brahmins, would work better for Dalits because the communities are not in direct conflict at the level of everyday life. He said: "This is not the case with communities like Yadavs, who have become land-owning classes only in recent times.

Kanshi Ram made these comments while justifying the BSP's first-ever alliance with the "upper caste" BJP in 1995. He said that one of the reasons for the collapse of the 1993 S.P- BSP alliance experiment was the conflict between Dalits and intermediate castes. Obviously keeping Kanshi Ram's views in mind, the BSP has made some advances towards the Brahmin community in every election in the past few years. In the last Assembly polls, the party gave the ticket to 26 Brahmins and got six of them elected. In the 2004 Lok Sabha polls it gave the ticket to six Brahmins and got one of them elected. This process got a fillip after the last Lok Sabha polls.

The Brahmin community in the State was veering towards the Congress immediately after the 2004 Lok Sabha elections and the defeat of the BJP. But large sections of the community realised that the Congress was not making much progress in building up a good organisation in Uttar Pradesh, despite being in power at the Center. These sections were ready to gravitate towards any party that would provide them with a core vote base so that they could add this to their individual support base and get elected to positions of power. "This is when the BSP leadership saw a chance to make quick political capital using the community and started wooing them," a senior Congress leader pointed out.

The fact that the rainbow social coalition of the Congress that helped the party hold sway over Uttar Pradesh politics for nearly four decades after Independence consisted mainly of the upper castes, Muslims and Dalits is clearly a factor that has been taken into account by the BSP leadership. Until the last elections, it received large chunks of the Dalit vote and a significant segment of the Muslim vote, but only a minuscule portion — less than 5 per cent of the upper caste vote. According to a senior BSP leader, the party is confident that it can dramatically alter equations even if it is able to garner one–tenth of the total upper caste vote.

Time alone can tell whether the calculations of the BSP leadership will yield the expected results. But there is little doubt that the Brahmin rally has pumped a new energy into the party's vote enhancing tactics.

Leadership right from the centre to the village level, is presently engaged in casting a spell on every major caste group. If the congress (I) organizes a Gujjar rally in a small town of Haryana, the Lok Dal leadership of the State inducts the Gujjar leader in the council of ministers and then calls a Brahmin Sammelan in another town to out do the rival. India's policy of compensatory or protective discrimination has given birth to scheduled caste and backward class politics. Reservation of civil jobs and legislative positions has certainly had the effect of increasing substantially the number of untouchables in positions of power and influence. It has also helped some of the ablest, or most advanced, untouchable members to enter the charmed circle of the Indian elite. But their organizations like the Dalits Sangharsa Samit are not satisfied. They are critical of the scheduled castes M.P.'s and MLA.'s and others in high positions for not helping the low placed members of the community. It is a great disappointment to them that they do not have the leader of the caliber and status of Dr. Ambedkar who may advance their interests more effectively and successfully. Their dissatisfaction with the scheduled castes elite is genuine because most of the untouchables despite legislation, the expenditure of millions of rupees and over three decades of federal and state efforts to improve their economic and social position remain desperately poor, semi-literate or illiterate and are subject to brutal discrimination and economic exploitation.

13

Caste in Contemporary India

There is a considerable disagreement among scholars over the influence of caste on the Indian society. Some well known sociologists and political scientists (Bailey, Mayer and Rajni Kothari) have described it as one of the major integrative elements of the Indian social structure. It has been perceived by some others as a bane, as an institution that is particularly depressive of social integration and economic development. According to Dr. Radhakrishnan, 'The occupational rationality of the caste system has gradually lost its earlier validity. Caste has ceased to be a social evil, but has become a political and administrative evil. Indeed, within the framework of modernization and political change, caste has taken on new dimensions and has also acquired a new emphasis. Local caste groups have been 'stretched' into caste associations and federations, regional political parties and blocs within state Congress. They are a means of pursuing political power, social status and economic interest. That apart, caste is evident everywhere, and at all levels of electoral process: the selection of candidates, the campaign, voting behaviour, and the formation of ministries. Unfortunately, the caste consciousness is on the increase. Never before has there been so much emphasis on caste-Jat and non-Jat, Reddi and Kama, Rajput and Bhumihar, Lingayat and Vokkaliga, Harijan and non-Harijan — as there is today. The top leaders may proclaim the goal of a casteless society, but the newly enfranchised rural masses know only the language of traditional politics which turns about caste.

Though caste is negating the democratic ideals, no political party, not even the Communist, is immune from its influence. Not many years ago, Jaya Parkash lamented that 'the caste had become most important political party in India'. Our experience of the Indian politics suggests that the right thinking politicians want caste and communal animosities to disappear, at the same time they are aware of the vote-catching power of caste. This puts them in a real dilemma, but to the common run of politicians it is an opportunity.

Caste has stimulated new and reinforced old varieties of factionalism. It works powerfully in favour of regionalism and against national integration. The country has seen hundreds of horrible incidents, including cases of murder, rape and torture, having all the trappings of a caste feud. To some, caste is worse than provincialism. Yet, the modern caste associations have enabled the members of middle and lower castes to find a basis for self-esteem and to win social esteem. As a result they have contributed to structural change by helping to level the ritually based social hierarchy of the caste system. At the same time, they have contributed to the success of political democracy by providing the basis of communication, representation and leadership and by linking the masses to the new democratic political process.

Some sociologists hold the view that caste is now not as dominant a social force as it used to be thirty or forty years before. Political power has to some extent detached itself from caste. General awareness and egalitarian norms have gradually eroded the caste loyalties. They have been weakened also by rapid industrialization, secular education and improved means of transportation and communication which have helped to cut across caste and sectional lines. Professor M.N. Srinivas does not agree with this view. He believes that development of communication, the spread of education and literacy, and rising prosperity have contributed, not to the disintegration of caste, but to its strengthening.

Should the caste be then abolished? Dr. V.K.R.V. Rao is not in favour of its abolition. He believes that caste has deep historical roots and serves the purpose of social grouping in an otherwise vast and heterogeneous population. Hence the best course under the circumstances is to cut down caste to its correct size and expel it from the political and economic arena where interested leaders have sought to use it for their power politics, individual aggrandizement and personal enrichment.

It is quite obvious that being a member of a caste or subcaste does not have the same meaning today for all individuals everywhere, if it ever did in the past; nor do caste sanctions operate with in the same force in all sections of Indian society. We have seen how the social reformers and the Indian Nationalists broke down the barriers of caste, particularly with respect to inter-dining and inter-marriage. We have seen how education industrialization, communication and urbanization have removed the connection between caste and occupation. We have further seen how the equal opportunity of education has provided a number of individuals of all castes to rise up in the social scale and how the Indian constitution as well as the untouchability Offences Act of 1955 and the Hindu Marriage Act of 1956 have completely removed all legal disabilities with respect to untouchability and with respect to intermarriage. We may now consider the net effect of all these drastic social changes in contemporary India.

It must be said that as far as the Hindu is concerned whether in the village or in the city, he has accepted all these changes, though not in a docile way. But he continues his life as a member of his caste group little bothered by the removal of the various legal disabilities.

It is sometimes said that, the underlying structure of caste remains what it was, and that if there are changes in caste practice, they are superficial and confined to a handful of urban or educated, or westernized individuals who are in any caste not truly representative of Indian society and culture. Thus, caste cannot possibly have the same meaning or the same legitimacy for all the individual members of such a large and diverse population. There is all the difference in the world between a senior member of the Kolkata or Mumbai bar and a small-town advocate; or between the research scientist in the Indian Institute of Science and the science teacher in a mofussil college.

European and American visitors to India often remark that when they ask educated Indians about caste, they are told that it does not exist any more. It would be a mistake to think that this is always an act of conscious deception. There is certainly an element of self-deception here, and we must ask why this form of self-deception is so commonly encountered. Of course, educated Indians know that caste exists, but they are unclear and troubled about what it means for them as members of a society, that is a part of modern world. No one can say that it is easy to give a clear and consistent account of the meaning and significance of caste in India today.

Whether he is a Brahmin or a non-Brahmin or a Harijan, caste endogamy is a living institution because the Indians as a whole, whether they are Hindus or Muslims or Christians, accept the principles of arranged marriages. It is true that there are several instances of inter-caste marriages-sometimes in defiance of the family, but often with the concurrence and approval of the members of the family. Mere inter-caste marriage by itself does not alter the caste affiliations. Similarly, though the Hindus as a whole, with very few exceptions among the orthodox people, now practice interdining, this does not affect the practice of caste system. Caste continues as an institution because it provides for a sense of identity with a larger group and a sense of security. The kinship relation is also a very strong factor in the life of an Indian. His attachment to his relatives is so strong that neither affiliation with a political group nor living a thousand or more miles away from home town or home village affects the strength of his kin affiliation.

At the time of independence, most reflective Indians felt that they had come to a watershed. It was upto them to seize and turn the country's advantage. They had a new constitution, a new five year plan, and then felt that, given the will power, they could do many things to bring about justice, equality, growth and well being for the people of India. Certain things needed to be put out of the way in order to achieve these objectives: poverty, hunger, malnutrition, illiteracy, ignorance and superstition. The caste system towards counted among the obstacles in the way of progress. Certainly, it would be fair to say that those who fashioned the constitution and the plans did not wish to give a new lease of life to caste.

The Indian perception of caste at the time of independence had been shaped, at least to some extent, by the dialectic between the colonial and the nationalist views regarding its place in the present and future society of India. For the Indian intellectual, it had become a matter of pride to confute the colonial view that, however eloquently they might talk about democracy and development, Indians were and would remain under the grip of caste with its exclusiveness, its hierarchy and its ineluctable fragmentation of civil society.

Since the Indian intelligentsia is today most troubled about the hierarchical distinctions of caste, it needs to be emphasized that in the past and up to the middle of the nineteenth century, those distinctions were, at least among the Hindus, acknowledged, upheld and reinforced by law, religion and morality. Things began to change there after, as a result of the British presence as well as the Indian response to it.

Caste undoubtedly exists in contemporary India and it does not, however, exist as a complete system any more, but if the phrase be permitted-as a truncated system.

Describing the changes which have taken place in the Hindu society in the last 30 years, K. Santanam writes, " I may stay my own personal experience. Coming from an orthodox Brahmin family in south India, I have a full experience of caste and untouchability as they were in the first decade of this century and as they are now. During my boyhood days, the vaishnavite Brahmins of South India would not dine even with samrat Brahmins. There was no question of their eating or associating with non Brahmins. Today, excepting the remote villages, the taboo against interdining or other forms of association has almost disappeared. My sons have been living in hostels with members of all castes and in fact they do not know the caste of their hostel mates. I have attended innumerable Congress conferences during these 20 years and have not found in them any distinction of caste or untouchability ever observed."

Thus, though social life in India has been revolutionized, still one can not say with any confidence that caste is not with us. It is there and probably will continue to be there in the future.

The question of caste morality is more difficult to dispose of briefly, for the evidence is often unclear and sometimes contradictory. One of its principal component was the caste into which he was born, to abide by its customs, to adhere to its style of life and to pursue the occupation allotted to it. Perhaps that sense of obligation, though not easily articulated, is still quite strong among cultivators, artisans and others in the rural areas. But it has weakened considerably in the urban areas. The compulsions of occupation operate rather differently in the different sectors of the Indian economy. Among engineers, doctors, scientists, civil servants, and managers, the obligation to one's occupation exists independently of the obligation to one's caste and to some extent displaces it. The school teacher, the clerk or the electrician no longer feels very strongly that he was a duty to encourage his offspring to persevere in his own occupation or the occupation of his forefathers as the village blacksmith, carpenter of potter might have felt in the past.

It is often said that no matter how loudly Hindus might proclaim their indifference or even hostility to caste, when it comes to marriage, all of them educated and uneducated, urban and rural, professional and peasant-turn to caste. Though caste may continue to operate in the field of social relations with in the homes and the principle of endogamy persists, the Hindu as a citizen is not hampered by these limitations. At home as well as in his work place, the Hndu-behaves like a citizen of the world. Further the caste taboos and discrimination do operate to a considerable extent in the rural areas. However, the caste system appears to persist in spite of all the changes in it and in the social system-neither modern education, nor modern economics, nor globalization, nor westernization, nor modern politics appear to have the strength to destroy it.

It will be of little value to argue about the decline in the legal, religious and moral basis of caste. One hears both kinds of arguments among the intelligentsia today: some say that intercaste marriages are now quite common while others maintain that they are rare and exceptional. One can get a good sense of the diversity of the categories at play by looking at the matrimonial advertisements in the Sunday news papers. These advertisements are classified, but not according to any single or consistent plan. The categories of caste are very prominent in these advertisement;

one should not be misled, however, because caste is frequently indicated, directly or indirectly, even under cosmopolitan. But then again some one may indicate his own caste, in case the party finds it relevant, even if he writes, 'caste, dowry no bar', to show that he does not regard it as relevant for himself.

The operation of caste along with language and religion in the political arena has led some to speak in a rather inclusive sense of 'ethnic groups', 'ethnic identities' and 'ethnic loyalties'. Srinivas has recently been quoted as saying, "In the future, too, caste will remain a predominant feature of Indian life. But it will be conceived more in terms of ethnicity. The movement from caste as varna to caste as ethnic group has been seen by some as the "substantialisation of caste." This may be some what misleading in so far as the notion of substance conveys a sense of homogeneity, whereas in fact each caste is becoming progressively differentiated in terms of occupation, education and income, clearly, some sifts are taking place in the meanings that people assign to caste. When journalists and political commentators refer to caste as ethnic groups, they have in mind not so much hierarchical distinctions of status as differences in bargaining power and in life chances in general.

Contemporary Indian life provides numerous occasions for the play of status in the factory, in the office, in hospitals, in laboratories and; in banks; in work and outside work; in both public and private places. The social world of the professional, the civil servant and the executive in the large metropolitan city is different from the social world of the village or even the small town. It would be rash to declare that the city is less animated by a concern for status than the village, and indeed, from the villager's point of view, the case may appear to be the opposite. That apart, the definition of status, its symbolic form and its social expression are not the same for the two.

In addition to caste, the things that count for status in the sections of society are education, occupation and income and the sub-cultures of the profession, the office and the association. The latter are by no means on unrelated to caste in the traditional sense, but they can hardly be regarded merely as aspects or expressions of it. The social world created by education, occupation and income, the office, the firm, the law court and the laboratory cuts across the social world of caste. The social circle of the Brahmin judge, diplomat, engineer, civil servant or manager is not the same as that of the Brahmin clerk, school teacher or cook. Particularly among the higher occupational strata many relationships are formed that cut across caste, as may be easily seen from the patterns of residence in large metropolitan cities where housing goes directly with occupation and income and only indirectly with caste. There are, to be sure, many continuities and linkages between the new status distinctions prominent among the intelligentsia and the old ones based largely on considerations of purity and pollution. Different criteria of status, different symbols of distinction and different strategies of exclusion now coexists in various sectors of Indian society.

We do not believe that caste has disappeared or is likely to disappear from even the sections of society; but shifts are taking place in the meaning and legitimacy of social relationship and social activities among many members of it. Evidence of some positive attachment to caste may be found in almost every sector of Indian society, among doctors, lawyers and scientists, and not to speak of administrators, managers and businessman. The statement from educated Indians that caste does not exist any more should be taken at face value. It is easy enough to show that caste has both a positive and negative significance for many members of contemporary Indian society.

In 1990 Indian intellectuals became deeply divided over the significance of caste on the issue of implementations of Mandal Commission recommendations. The division was over an issue of policy, that of caste quotas in education and employment. It has been said that those who opposed quotas minimized the significance of caste, some deliberately. But it must not be assumed that those who supported quotas thought that caste was a good thing which ought to be strengthened; on the contrary, they said that caste was an evil but believed that the best way of doing away with in the long run was by having quotas in short run. At any rate, those who supported the quotas belonged to diverse castes, and Indian intellectuals, who are predominantly of upper caste, both supported and opposed the quotas.

In certain contexts, caste might matter more for Harijan than for Brahmin intellectuals as race seems to do more for black that for white intellectuals in the united States. But this again would be a kind of reversal of the traditional order where caste matters were ultimately the responsibility of the upper and not the lower castes. If we are to understand what is happening to caste in contemporary India, we will have to look for new types of data, devise new concepts and above all, approach the subject with a more open mind that does not seek either to ignore the distinctive features of Indian society or to maximize the difference between India and the west.

14

Steps to Check Casteism

There is every need to check the role of casteism in Indian politics. For this purpose the following steps can be suggested:

Popularization of secularism as the best way of life. Secularization of political culture, effective and objective formulation and implementation of development plans for all castes and the adoption of a mature political approach and a national vision by all political elites can together go a long way in the meeting the menace of casteism in India. Steps should be taken towards the elimination of socioeconomic injustice against the scheduled castes and scheduled tribes. The spread of education only make them cautious against the evils of casteism. A well organized and value based system of education will train the minds of people. Education can alone help to develop national character. Economic imbalance and property of certain caste groups act as a serious obstacle to national integration. The backward classes and the weaker sections of society should be made for their upliftment and prosperity. There should be balanced growth among the castes. Culture helps to establish uniformity and develop a set of values which may be regarded as the national goals. In spite of differences among the castes, there is a sense of cultural unity throughout the country. The political party should not encourage caste tendencies. Anti-caste activities of politicians and political parties pose a danger to national integration. All steps should be taken to combat the forces of casteism.

Both Governmental and nongovernmental organizations have great responsibility in this matter. M.V. Mathur also called upon the political parties to adopt a non-caste and non-regional approach to political issues. Moonis Raza feels that the historical injustice done to the tribes, which were pushed into 'refuse' areas in the interior of the country i.e. Madhya Pradesh, Andhra Pradesh and Bihar, must be done away with and they should be given land and other facilities for preserving their identity and develop their interest. Casteism should be treated as a social evil and strong social movements against casteism should be encouraged. The mass media should highlight the uselessness of caste distinctions.

Another condition essential is that the people should possess, "A genuine sense of nationalism which transcends the barriers of language, religion, caste and tribe. Social justice is another important strategy against casteism. *Social justice* implies that people should enjoy maximum freedom with reasonable social control in the best interest of the community. Social justice also implies a balanced society. It protects minority interests, removes social evils, protects downtrodden and weaker sections of the society. Thus the society should not recognize any differences based on caste or creed. Untouchability has been made an offence punishable by law under the constitution. It is true that it does not create any special privilege for anyone. Yet it was hailed as a great fundamental right, a charter of deliverance to one-sixth of Indian population from perpetual subjugation and despair, from perpetual humiliation and disgrace.

The nature of the problems of the untouchables has changed during the last fifty years. The practice of untouchability has practically disappeared in trains, buses, offices, schools, factories and other such public places. The traditional rigidity with which it was practised in day to day life has declined considerably only in towns and cities. But even in many villages the evils of untouchability still persists. The Government should promise to eradicate untouchability within a stipulated time. More efforts to create strong public opinion against those who disobey the law and economic uplift of the Harijans are essential to achieve appreciable practical results. Caste associations and caste federations which have been officially recognized, should be banned in the political process.

India is a multiethnic society in which there are a large number of ethnic groups. These groups very enormously insofar as self-conscious awareness of common identity is concerned. In some parts of the country the awareness of common identity is the root cause of caste prejudices. The religious manifestations and greater self awareness of religious communities are generally taken as antithetical to secularism. It is believed that there can be no real progress towards the goal of secularism unless the country begins building up a composite culture and moves towards socioeconomic integration.

Concrete steps should be taken to prevent the use of caste for electoral ambitions of political parties. No one should exploit such traditional institution and values as caste, religion, sect, ethnic membership in order to secure vote.

The tragic inability of the high castes to live in peace and harmony with the untouchables is indeed distressing. The minority Harijans in every village make some adjustments with the dominant ethos of the majority high caste Brahmins and Kshatriyas. Therefore, both the caste groups should take uncompromising attitude towards each other.

Rajani Kothari says, "Apart from the divisive and factional aspects of the caste, there is a cohesive element of caste that should be looked into. When a nation is changing so fast and when tensions are generated at very high pitch, when we face problems that can not be solved, when the gap between performance and expectation is increasing, when all this is happening, there is a great need of social structure which absorb a lot of these tensions for the individuals. The caste system does precisely this. This should not be taken as a plea for revival of the caste system. The objective is only to emphasize that it is a unique feature in India that the prevailing social structure allows us to proceed with mass programmes without creating the usual features of an amorphous mass upon which some adventurist or demagogue can work."

F.G. Bailey has rightly said that, "caste is not a principle by which political economic groups, are recruited nor does it organize relations between political groups but it is an organizing principles with in social groups."

Another step to check casteism is the encouragement of inter-caste marriages. The great epic of Hindu society, the Mahabharata also describes a number of intercaste marriages. Santanu, the progenitor of the Kuru-Pandavas first married Ganga and later Satyavati, a fisher-woman, both outside his caste. Manu has classified and named the offspring of anuloma (higher varna man marrying a lower varna woman) and pratiloma (lower varna marrying a higher varna women) marriages and all possible combinations of the marriages, indicating that during his time inter-Varna marriages were prevalent.

In the present society inter-caste marriages were very rare, because in an agricultural society following caste system and arranged marriages, it is very difficult for a man or a women to marry outside the caste. However, with the increase of women's education, there have been many inter-caste marriages. Inter-caste marriage is one of the best ways against casteism. Therefore the government as well as non-governmental organizations should encourage inter-caste marriages for the emergence of a society based on equal status of caste.

The reservation policy must be periodically reviewed and suitably modified. The time has come to decide whether it is going to continue forever or it is to be stopped after a definite date. The issue must be decided at the national level and through a national consensus. It should not be politicized any further.

Last but not the least, the inner unity of all the castes i.e., their shared and common values should be used as foundations for projecting the composite culture of our people.

Such steps can help us fight the menace of casteism. Casteism has been a national menace and All Indian must come forward to untidily fight the forces of casteism which have been putting a grave strain on the health of our nation.

Select Bibliography

Aggarwala RN, *National Movement and Constitutional Development of India,* Metropolitan Book, Delhi, 1956.

Almond GA and Powell, GB, Comparative polities. A Developmental Approach, Amerind, New Delhi 1972.

Appadorai A, *Essays in Indian Politics and Foreign Policy,* Vikas Publications, Delhi, 1971.

Atal Yogesh, *Changing Frontiers of Caste,* National Publishing House, Delhi, 1979.

Ayyappan A, *Social Revolution in a Kerala Village,* Asia Publishing House, Bombay, 1965.

Bailey FG, *Politics and Social Change in Orissa,* Oxford University Press, Bombay, 1959.

Beteille Andre, *Caste Old and New,* Asia Publishing House, Bombay, 1967.

Bendix R and Lipset, SM, (eds), *Class, Status and Power, Social Stratification in Comparative Perspective,* Routledge and Kegan Paul, London, 1970.

Bhatt Anil, *Caste, Class and Politics,* Manohar Book Service, New Delhi, 1975.

Bachal VM, *Peoples Mandate* (eds), Sri Mudran Mandir, Pune, 1989.

Bhatkal Ram Das, *Snakes and Ladders, India Votes: 1996* (eds), Popular Prakashan, Mumbai, 1996.

Bhalla RP, *Elections in India (1950-72),* S. Chand and Co, New Delhi, 1973.

Blunt, E.A.H., *The Caste System of Northern India,* S. Chand and Company, 1969.

Barber Bernard, *Social Stratification: A Comparative Analaysis of Structure and Process,* Harcourt, New York, 1957.

Bavadam Lyla, Opportunistic Overtures, *Frontline,* April 11, 2003, pp. 46-48.

Bose N.K, *Culture and Society in India,* Vikas Publishing House, Delhi, 1970.

Bottomore T.B, *Classes in Modern Society,* Allen and Unwin, London, 1971.

Brass Paul, R, *Language, Religion and Politics in North India,* Vikas, New Delhi, 1974.

Brecher Michael, *Political Leadership in India—An Analysis of Elite Attitudes,* Vikas Publications, Delhi, 1969.

Carolyn Milliot, Caste and faction among dominant caste, The Reddis and Kammas in Andhra in Rajani Kothari (Ed.), caste in Indian politics, Orient longman, New Delhi, 1971.

Chattopadhya, S., *Social Life in Ancient India,* Academic Publishers, Calcutta, 1965.

Cole G.D.H., *Studies in Class Structure,* Routledge and Kegan Paul, London, 1995.

Das Baishnav Charan, Mahanty Amarendra, & Das Mandakini, *Democracy, Nation Building and Ideologies,* Modern Publisher, New Delhi, 2003.

Das HH & Choudhary BC, *Political Sociology,* Vidyarthi Vawan, Brahmapur, Orissa, 1986.

Dahl Robert A, *Modern Political Analysis,* Prentice Hall, New Delhi, 1965.

Damodaran Asok K and Ansari M Javed, Bihar Rubbed *Out, India Today,* February 22,1999.

Dumont Louis, *Homo Hierachicus,* Vikas Publication, New Delhi, 1970.

Dutta N.K., *Origin and Growth of Caste in India,* Vol.-1, The Book Company, Calcutta, 1931.

Ghai K.K., *Democracy, Nation Building and Ideologies,* Kalyani Publishers, Ludhiana, 2004.

Ghurye G.S., *Caste and Class in India,* Popular Publication, Bombay, 1950.

Ghurye G.H., *Caste, Class and Occupation,* Popular Publication, Bombay, 1961.

Gould H.A., Towards A Jati Model for Indian Politics, *Economic & Political Weekly,* February, 1969, pp. 291-297.

Hardgrave R.L., *The Dravidian Movement,* Popular Prakashan, Bombay, 1965.

Hartmann Horst, *Political Parties in India,* Meenakshi Prakashan, 1971.

Hutton, *Caste in India,* Oxford University Press, Bombay, 1946.

Iqbal Narain, *The Rural Elite in An Indian State; A Case Study of Rajasthan,* Monohar Book Company, New Delhi, 1976

Iqbal Narain, (eds) *State Politics in India,* Meenakshi Prakashan, Meerut, 1976

Jha Chetakar, Caste and Religion in Indian Politics, in Romesh Thapars (Ed.), *Tribe, Caste and Religion in India,* Seminar Publication, New Delhi, 1977.

Kameswar Choudhary, Caste in Politics, *The Times of India,* August 12, 1988.

Kasyap Subhash (eds.), *Elections Electoral Reforms in India,* Sterling Publishers and distributers, New Delhi, 1971.

Keer D., *Dr Amedkar,* Popular Prakashan, Bombay, 1962.

Kothari Rajani, Introduction in Rajani Kothari (Ed.), *Caste in Indian Politics,* Orient Longman, New Delhi, 1971.

Kothari Rajani (Ed.), *Party Politics and Election Studies,* Allied Publishers, New Delhi, 1967.

Kothari Rajani, *Politics in India,* Sangam Press, Poona, 1970.

Kothari Rajani, *Party Politics in India,* Orient Longman, New Delhi, 1970.

Kolenda Paulin, *Caste in Contemporary India,* Rawat Publication, Jaipur, 1984.

Kuppuswamy B, *Social Change in India,* Bikash Publishing House, Gaziabad, 1979.

Menon C Achuta (Eds.), Renaissance Movement in Kerala, in, *For An Indian Model* C Achuta Menon Foundation, Thiruvanantapuram, 1993.

Mahanty Gopinath, Cultural Heritage of Ganjam, State Level Vyasakavi Fakir Mohan Smruti Sansad, Bhubaneswar, 2004.

Menon V K W, *India Since Independence from the Preamble to the Present,* S Chand and Co, New Delhi, 1970.

Mukerji Debasish, The Resilent Brahmin, *The Week,* November 10, 1969, pp. 36,37.

Naqvi Saeed, *The Last Brahmin Prime Minister,* Har Anand Publisher, 1996.

Oomen TK, *Social Structure and Politics, Studies in Independent India,* Hindustan Publishing Corporation, 1984.

Panikkar K M, *Hindu Society at Crossroads,* Asia Publishing House, Bombay, 1961.

Palmer Norman D, *Elections and Political Development—The South Asian Experiences,* Vikash Publishing, New Delhi, 1976.

Prabhu P H, *Hindu Social Organisation,* Popular Prakashan, Bombay, 1963.

Prasad Narmadeswa, The Myth of the Caste System, Samajha Prakashan, Patna, 1957.

Rajgopalchari C, *Mahabharat,* Bharatiya Vidya Bhawan, New Delhi, 1952.

Ramachandra Rajesh, Affirm Arise, *Outlook,* 14 March, 2005, p. 24.

Ramakrishnan Venkitesh, A New Caste Formula, *Frontline,* July 1, 2005, pp. 27, 28.

Rout B C & Mahapatra M K, *New Rudiments of Political Science,* Nalanda, Cuttack, 2004.

Sivanath Sastri, *History of Bramho Samaj,* Vol-1, R Chatterjee, Calcutta, 1917.

Sharma Anuradha, *Caste in India,* Indian Publishers Distributers, New Delhi, 1998.

Singh Gopal and Sharma H L, *Reservation Politics in India,* Deep and Deep Publications, New Delhi, 1995.

Singh Y, *Social Stratification and Change in India,* Manohar Publications, New Delhi, 1977.

Sikri S L., *Indian Govt. and Politics,* Kalyani Publishers, New Delhi, 2002.

Sharma K L, *Essays on Social Stratification,* Rawat Publications, Jaipur, 1980.

Singh K K, *Pattern of Caste Tensions,* Asia Publishing House, Bombay, 1967.

Sirisikar V M, *Political Behaviour in India,* Manaktala and Sons, Bombay, 1965.

Sirisikar V M, *Tribe, Caste and Politics,* in Romesh (Ed.), Thaper *Tribe Caste and Religion in India,* Seminar Publication, New Delhi, 1977.

Srinivas M N, *Caste in Modern India,* Asia Publishing House, New Delhi, 1962.

Srinivas M N, *Social Change in Modern India,* Orient Longman, New Delhi, 1972.

Srinivas M N, *Religion and Society Among the Coorgs of South India,* Asia Publishing House, Bombay, 1952.

Srinivas M N, *Indian Social Structure,* Hindustan Publishing Corporation, New Delhi, 1980.

Swami Praveen, A Shrine and A Struggle, *Frontline,* July 4, 2003, pp. 3940.

Swaminathan, S, Signs of Change, *Frontline,* August 16, 2002, pp. 34-35.

Swaminathan, S, Disempowering Dalits, *Frontline,* May 20,2005, p. 39.

Swaminathan, S, Intolerance and Resistance, *Frontline,* July 2, 2004, pp. 44-45.

Swaminathan, S, Killing For Caste Honour, *Frontline,* September 12, 2003, pp. 38, 39.

Verma S P, Iqbal Narain and Associates, *Voting Behaviour in a Changing Society,* National Publishing House, New Delhi, 1973.

Vivekananda: *India and Her Problems,* Advaita Ashram, Calcutta, 1963.

Viswanathan, S, Conversion as Protest, *Frontline,* July 2, 2004, pp. 44-45.

Index

Sidanis
8620
29/08/09